THE ESSENTIAL KIRBY CANON

20 Years of Shooting From the Hip

at the Salt Lake Tribune

Robert Kirby

ZION Book Works

An Imprint of Leicester Bay Books

Salt Lake City

Zion BookWorks
3877 Leicester Bay
South Jordan UT 84095

www.zionbookworks.com

First Edition by Zion BookWorks: 2014 --
ISBN-13: 978-0692266083
ISBN-10: 0692266089

Kindle Edition: 2014

Cover illustration by Pat Bagley

The Essential Kirby Canon is Book #6 in the
MORMON HUMOR COLLECTION
from
Zion BookWorks

ALSO BY ROBERT KIRBY

Happy Valley Patrol
Brigham's Bees
Dark Angel
Sunday of the Living Dead
Wake Me for the Resurrection
Pat & Kirby Go To Hell
Family Home Screaming
Kirby Soup for the Soul
End of Watch: Utah's Murdered Police Officers, 1858-2004

For Irene,
who hasn't divorced me
yet.

ACKNOWLEDGMENTS

No newspaper columnist is ever successful without a good editor. Opinions differ wildly on what makes an editor good, but for my own purposes it is someone interested in and capable of saving me from myself.

Deserving of particular gratitude is Lisa Carricaburu, my editor from 2005-2014. With her I had a firm governess and a great collaborator. It was a personal calamity when she left the paper for another job. I still miss her.

But I was left in the good editor hands of Sheila McCann, whose gracious advice and pleasant exterior I suspect hides the soul of a ruthless deadline tyrant. Lisa knew what I needed.

There were others before them. I would not have lasted long as a writer but for the efforts of Jay Shelledy, Terry Orme, Tim Fitzpatrick, Peg McEntee, Dave Noyce, and Peggy Fletcher-Stack.

Then there is Sonny Dyle, a close friend without whose reckless companionship I would have fewer scars today but also considerably less to write about.

Finally there is my family, whose tolerance at being exposed in print helped get me here in the first place.

Table of Contents

1. Warning for Would-Be Writers   1

2. Qualifications for Solomon   4

3. This Might Be The Place   7

4. Digging Up the Past   10

5. Raising Grandson Hell   13

6. High Speed Bowling   15

7. Explosive Pest Control   18

8. Shocking Police Research   21

9. Fire On the Mountain   23

10. Restitution Solution   26

11. The Legacy of Boom   29

12. Big Bottom Blues   31

13. Emergency Repair Kit   34

14. Rules of the Road   37

15. Garbage Sale   40

16. 'Til We Beat Again   42

17. Training for the Olympics   45

18. Checking Out the Other Side   48

19. Relief Society Application   50

20. Mormon Meany Matters   53

21. Getting into Conference   56

22. Street Screeching   58

23. Should Have Been a Cowboy   61

24. Learning and Loss   64

25. Tavaputs Plateau Oysters   66

26. Going Greek in Utah   69

27. Suiting up for the Devil   72

28. Zion Trek Fashions   74

29. Church in the Mean Time   77

30. Sage Advice Rebellion   80

31. Church Snacking   83

32. And I'm a Mormon…   86

33. A Dog's Life   89

34. Weinermobile Driving   91

35. Collagen for Dessert   94

36. Life Round the Bend   96

37. Scouting with the Master   100

38. His Holiness The Kirb   103

39. Talking Turkey Trash   106

40. Waiting on Eternity   109

41. No Place to Park City   112

42. Suburban Water Torture   115

43. Right Person, Wrong Place   117

44. Coping with the Faithful   120

45. Ringing For Help   123

46. Excommunication for the Dead   125

47. Home Teaching Lessons   128

48. Homecoming at Skyline   131

49. Keeping Your Own Faith   134

50. My Particles of Faith   137

Author Bio   139

INTRODUCTION

Twenty years. Damn. Where did that go? If the next 20 years go that fast, I should keep this brief.

My first column in *The Salt Lake Tribune* ran on April 24, 1994. I was still working for another newspaper at the time, one that didn't appreciate my lampooning Utah's predominant culture and would eventually fire me when I wouldn't stop.

I couldn't stop. I'm a part of that culture but also a strong adherent of David Bouchier's claim that "all tribes have strange customs, and the writer's job is to become an anthropologist to his or her own tribe."

After getting fired, I free-lanced as a columnist for three years until *The Salt Lake Tribune* hired me full time. I found a home at the Tribune

In the beginning I was just looking for a little fun. That and maybe some get back for a lifetime of really bad Sunday school lessons and worse legislature. It was only later that I realized the imperative nature of being able to laugh at ourselves.

If you've made it this far, I should warn you about what comes next. In the 50 selected columns that follow understand that I'm not making fun of God or your sacred cow. I'm making fun of you. If you can't tell the difference, you're precisely the reason it needs doing.

Robert Kirby -- October 7, 2014

1

Warning for Would-Be Writers

It's career day at the high school. In a couple of hours, I will be teaching a bunch of teenagers everything I know about being a writer. Should take all of about, oh, five minutes.

Who really knows what they want to be when they grow up? Becoming a writer certainly never occurred to me. If scholastic endeavor was any indication, I was destined for a long career of smoking under a set of bleachers.

When I was five, I wanted to be a fire truck. Not a fireman, the actual truck. As dumb as it sounds, this was merely the first in a long series of attempts to be something I couldn't possibly be.

Between fire truck and writer, I tried a lot of things. At one time or another I have washed cars, bagged groceries, caught rats, soldiered, preached, built houses, thrown people in jail, and reported the news. Hated all of them.

Wait, that's not entirely true. I sort of liked catching rats at Ft. Douglas. The pay was bad but I was good at it. I had plans to parlay my expertise into a series of lucrative McRat franchises but Uncle Sam had other ideas. Turned out the rats belonged to him, and, incidentally, so did I.

So who am I to suggest anything to high school kids? The last thing any parent or teacher should want is for a teenager to follow in my footsteps. The last thing I want is for them to become writers. Frankly, I don't hate anyone that bad.

Anyway, for what it's worth, here is what I know about writing. Granted, it's not much. Most of it I learned the hard way, this advice notwithstanding, so will you. If you want to save yourself a lot of pain, be a fire truck instead.

First, you have to be a little crazy to be a writer. That and maybe a bit arrogant. After all, it takes a certain amount of ego to presume that reasonably intelligent people will stop what they are doing to read something you wrote. Especially if you expect them to pay for the privilege.

There are writers and then there are writers. Tech, news, ad, fiction, there are lots of different kinds of writing. Self-important yawping to the contrary, one type isn't more noble than another. When pressed, a good writer will try them all.

Writers write, even when they don't publish. Basically this means that writing isn't something you think about as much as it is something you do. It's hour after hour of trying to sensibly arrange on paper the stuff that doesn't really make sense in your head. Do it long enough and eventually it comes even when you don't want it to.

Knowing how to write is less important than having something to write about. See the world, get hurt, hurt somebody, bleed, forgive. All worthwhile writing is based on hope and loss. In other words, stuff you still want to do, and stuff you wish you hadn't.

Get tough. Short of maybe nude dancing, nothing is more punishing to the ego than baring your soul on paper to strangers. The only way to conquer a fear of rejection is to get rejected, usually a lot. Do it enough and your skin will eventually stop anti-tank rounds.

Never discount dumb luck when it comes to success. Getting published in no way means you have arrived. Sometimes it means that an editor made a mistake. How it all works out is still largely up to you.

There you have it. Everything I know about being a writer. If nothing else, I hope that I've shown you the errors of my ways.

SLT - November 6, 1997

2   **Qualifications for Solomon**

The State Legislature has glutted itself. Couched in the kindest terms, the 2004 legislature was referred to as "positive" and even as "not a superstar" session.

These of course are just polite ways of saying that during the 45-day pecking of the public carcass no legislator was actually beaten to the point of incontinence.

In reality, the recent legislature was a gouging, snarling, backstabbing brawl worthy of the Medici. Ultraconservative gasbags tried to save us from ourselves, while liberal blowholes tried to save us from everything else.

Every year I maintain a hope that lawmakers will produce something we can all be proud of, a legislative session that shines as a beacon of hope to an already fractious state.

Alas, we end up with an idea that Utah would be better served if on the busiest day of the session we simply nailed the State Capitol doors shut and called in a fumigator.

What's the worst that could happen? OK, we would have to come up with a whole bunch of new legislators. How bad could that be?

Isn't there some kind of qualification to be a state legislator? There is to be a columnist. We have to correctly spell many three-letter words and cannot ever have been convicted of punching an editor before deadline. That's about it.

But legislators occupy the top Solomon slots in our state. We let some of the most self-important people around tell us how to live, with whom we can live, what to drink, where to drink it, and even how we choose to die.

So, it seems to me there should be better qualifications for the job than just being well heeled and connected. How about these?

KIRBY'S BILL FOR
MINIMUM LEGISLATIVE JOB QUALIFICATIONS

1. Must have been an elementary school teacher for at least two years. I recently spoke to a fifth grade class at Lone Peak Elementary. It was like trying to herd weasels with an air horn. No one who hasn't done it a lot should have any say in education funding.

2. One-year minimum street cop or emergency room experience. Someone who hasn't come home from a hard day at the office with pieces of traffic accident and homicide victims on them has no business lecturing the public about seat-belt use and capital punishment.

3. Five years experience living below the poverty line as a single parent. This one is a no-brainer. What do the scions of privilege know about welfare or even being a pregnant teenager?

4. Religion is a big sticking point in Utah. So, before serving as a legislator, one must faithfully practice a religion not his or her own (and of our choosing) for two years. Tell me that 24 months as a devout Rasta man wouldn't do certain legislators a world of good.

5. Two complete (and successful) seasons as a small farmer or rancher. Anyone who can profitably feed sheep and turkeys—two of God's dumbest animals next to the general public—must know something about careful cash management.

There you have it. Anyone with this kind of resume would not only deserve our vote, but we might even consider making them our king or queen.

SLT - March 6, 2004

3   This Might Be The Place

Recorded in my great-great-great-grandfather Korihor Kirby's journal are his feelings upon seeing Zion for the first time.

The year was 1855. Leaving Ohio in the spring, Grandpa Korihor made the arduous pioneer trek to Utah. On a late fall afternoon, the company paused near the spot where Brigham Young had previously identified the valley as "this is the place."

Apparently, the desert view was something of a shock to a guy from Ohio. That evening, an irate Grandpa Korihor wrote, "Somebody—I'm not saying who—is out of his #&@#! mind!"

I know exactly how he felt. I have my own "This Is The Place" monument. It's the dining room window of my parents' home in Holladay. That's where I got my first real glimpse of Utah more than 40 years ago.

My family trekked here in 1970, when events beyond our control forced us to abandon everything and head off to Zion in a covered (station) wagon.

On a warm February afternoon, we left friends and family in southern California. Driving all day, we arrived in Salt Lake in the middle of the freezing night. Because it was dark, all we saw initially were street lights and low clouds.

The following morning, I got up and looked out the

window. It wasn't what I saw that troubled me, but rather what I didn't see.

Noticeably absent were the things I had been forced to leave behind—the ocean, palm trees, Disneyland, my friends, and any semblance of normalcy.

"This place sucks," I prophesied.

And I was right, at least for a while. Actually, it was more like a long time than a while. It took about ten years before I completely got over being hauled off to someplace I didn't want to be.

Unless you were born here, Utah comes as a bit of a shock. Ironically, that includes Mormons who move here. This place is—different. It takes some serious getting used to, especially if you were perfectly comfortable where you were before.

Most newcomers don't journey to Zion because they want to. I doubt there are more than a handful of transplants here who suddenly got it into their heads to pull up stakes and move to the middle of the desert and Mormons.

More often than not it's because they were compelled here by a job, school, family, or something else they couldn't say no to. For my early Mormon ancestors, it was God. For my father (and more importantly me), it was the U.S. Army.

My friend Kathy moved here in 1990 when her husband was transferred. Her "this place sucks" moment came when she couldn't find a single person in her neighborhood to invite over for coffee.

Another friend's moment came when John realized that he could go for days at a time without seeing another black person.

If you can't change the place, the best you can hope for is to change your mind. Decades later, all three of us are still in

Utah. Only now, it's by choice.

John got married, Kathy found some friends, and I stopped thinking "this is the place" was somewhere else.

SLT - July 23, 2011

4 Digging Up The Past

Paleontology is way harder than it looks on TV. Smart people probably already know this. Last week, I drove 300 miles and sat in a hole all day to find it out.

TV paleontology is accomplished with small hammers, tiny brooms and lots of scientific blather. Occasionally a brilliant deduction is made. Everything is wrapped up in the space of 30-60 minutes minus commercials.

From my limited perspective, real paleontology amounts to far more digging and head scratching than a rational person enjoys. It appears to help if you also know how to argue, cuss, and speak Latin.

At any rate, this is how paleontologists find and classify dinosaur bones. On Friday, I did some of it with a team from the College of Eastern Utah. We dug up a brachiosaur, or at least the parts of it that we could find.

The team consisted of Jeff, Duane, Marvin, Nick and Bill. As the only professional paleontologist among us, Jeff was the boss of the dig. Not that this meant anything. He was also the craziest one in the bunch.

Even so, you can't beat a university education. I could bring something to Jeff and ask him to identify which part of the dinosaur it was. After careful examination, he could, with authority, say, "This I'm pretty sure is a bottle cap."

First, though, we had to get to a semi-secret location

known as PR2. Because paleontologists hate it when vandals and thieves help them with their work, I can only say that PR2 is located about an hour of really horrible road from Price.

The word brachiosaur literally means "arm lizard," a reference to its overly stout front legs. In terms of forearms, it was the Popeye of dinosaurs.

It might as well mean "big #%@&!" because all of its bones are enormous. An average brachiosaur stood four stories high and weighed more than Kirstie Allie.

Brachiosaur wasn't anywhere near as bright as Kirstie nor as agile. It had a brain about the size and acuity of a golf ball. According to my research, our particular brachiosaur lived during the Flintstones Period some 125 million years ago. It plodded mindlessly about eating and mating until it fell over dead in a swamp.

Over the years, the same thing happened to brachiosaur that happened to Congress. Nor is the analogy lost on what it takes to arrive at any sort of sense regarding their purpose. In either case much pounding and hollering.

We dug and picked and swept and grunted and eventually pried from the earth an actual brachiosaur butt bone. The scientific term is an "ischium." But Bill showed me a diagram of where it fit on the dinosaur. It's a butt bone.

Jeff was positively ecstatic. It was a marvelous ischium. No better ischium existed anywhere. I wouldn't know. Mainly because I never actually saw it. From what I saw, we covered a blob of rock in a larger blob of plaster, then hauled it out of the hole and heaved it into a truck.

Five hours later we had exposed another two dozen bones. The arrangement of bones says a lot about how a dinosaur died. In this case it appeared that our brachiosaur had run afoul of a roadside bomb. It was everywhere.

I learned a lot from the dig. Mainly I learned that journalism suits me better. There's no intelligent design argument in what I do.

SLT - October 10, 2005

5 Raising Grandson Hell

I was in Mesquite, Nevada, giving a nonsensical speech to a group from the U.S. Department of Agriculture when the call came that our daughter had gone into labor.

We left immediately, which also happened to be in the middle of the night and in our pajamas. Fortunately, the UHP was home in bed.

Even so, we got there too late. My grandson, a decidedly handsome devil, was born Thursday morning at Cottonwood Hospital. Mother and son are doing fine. The father, however, is still an idiot.

Missing the birth doesn't really bother me. I've seen it before and there's nothing magical about it. As Dave Barry once observed, it's like watching a wet St. Bernard trying to come in through the cat door.

Gage Robert Morgan looks like he was in a fight. His forehead sports a large purple bruise that medical professionals refer to as a "skid mark," a natural abrasion that comes from his sudden birth.

Now I need your advice. This is my first boy. All my experience with children, both as a father and a grandfather, has been with girls. I want to get it right. And this time there is a possibility that I can.

My wife and I have three daughters, one granddaughter, two female labrador retrievers, and a neutered cat. Except for two sons-in-law, the only bit of testosterone around here with my name on it has been me.

Being surrounded by estrogen, over the years I got used to not knowing what the hell was going on. Male thought and behavior in our home were regarded as mental illness.

Oh, shut up. One look at a bathroom inhabited entirely by women and it doesn't take a psychiatrist to tell that you aren't in your right minds either.

Now I have a blood ally and I plan to make the most of it. I went out immediately and picked up the basics: a bike, a football, a hammer, a subscription to Victoria's Secret, and a handgun (.45-caliber Colt Combat Commander).

NOTE: If you are incensed that I would buy a gun for a newborn, let's skip the part where you write me a letter expressing high moral outrage and go straight to the part where I tell you to stick it in your ear.

Raising a boy has to be different than raising girls. For starters, Gage and I will intuitively understand each other. We are both men.

He won't burst into tears if I point out how stupid it is to support a sports team for no other reason than their color coordination. And he will know that what is under the hood of a truck is more important than what kind of seat covers it has.

I already reinforced the shower curtain rod, which, ladies, believe it or not was intended for tougher duty than just drying pantyhose. Oh, and I warned the cat about the dryer.

What else? If there's something I'm missing, something absolutely essential to raising the complete boy, tell me. Hurry up. He's already four days old.

SLT - January 19, 2004

6 High Speed Bowling

Sonny and I have taken up bowling in a big way. I never realized just how much fun there is in a sport previously considered even more pointless than golf.

Granted, my experience with bowling had been limited to a few first dates and catching glimpses of it on TV where announcers discussed it in hushed, conspiratorial tones normally reserved for the clergy and criminals.

Everything changed when Sonny and I got our hands on a bowling ball cannon. Now bowling is interesting as well as important.

Cannon bowling works on the same principles as regular bowling, but now the lane is a mile long, the pins are trees, and a "strike" can be heard in the next county. Even further if you accidentally hit somebody important.

We acquired our "BB" gun through entirely legal means. We got it from a known arms dealer who specializes in high-end lunatic weaponry: Rick at Coaches Club Cannons.

In addition to bowling, CCC makes guns applicable to other sports. Who knew that golf, baseball, and tennis had whole other levels to them?

Bowling ball gunnery is not, as you may be thinking, just a sport. It's also hard scientific research. Don't tell me that you've never wondered whether a slightly used Radical ReAx competition ball could go clear through a stack of wooden pallets.

Well, it will. Not only that, it will keep on going through a fence AND an old shed for another 150 yards. You're welcome.

Like most sports, there is some risk to BB gunnery, not the least of which is to always remember where you parked, and to never "bowl" in the direction of civilization.

Bowling like this has changed my life. Where I once saw some things as onerous, I now see them as advantageous.

Yesterday, my daughter asked me to install a new washer and dryer in a laundry room the size of a coat closet. It took two hours of sweating and cursing to manhandle the old ones out, and the new ones in.

Finished, I was left with what to do with the old appliances. Where I once would have been thinking "a trip to the landfill" I now thought, "Cool targets."

With due caution, long practice and enough ammunition, it's possible to turn semi pro in bowling ball gunnery. Crazy Dave in Richfield challenged Sonny and me to a BB shootout in July. Best of three shots or until the cops come.

All of this brings me to the point of this column, which is a serious one. Practice can be expensive.

The primary difference between ordinary bowling and cannon bowling is that the former employs an automatic ball return.

At a bowling alley your ball is returned to you in a matter of seconds regardless of how much force you used to send it downrange. There's even a machine to polish up your ball if it gets a little scratched.

Cannon bowling is pretty much a one-way affair. When you send the ball on its way with a four ounce "release" of black powder, you aren't going to want it back. And that's assuming you can even find the damn thing.

So we need bowling balls. New or used, it doesn't matter. They all shoot the same. If you have that one you want to get rid of, let me know.

SLT - March 19, 2014

7   Explosive Pest Control

In the summer of 1963, a gopher burrowed into our backyard. My father offered me 25 cents to get rid of it.

I tried everything: BB gun, snare, garden hose, mousetrap, and even a special poison I concocted from insecticide, broccoli, and underarm deodorant. Nothing worked. I finally gave up.

A month later, I accidentally hit the gopher while mowing the lawn. The old man still paid up, but by then the damage was done. I knew that a rodent half the size of a Twinkie was smarter than I was. It set the tone for the rest of my life.

On Thursday, I finally decided to get some therapy. I followed around a pest control squad that uses a contraption called a Rodenator.

NOTE: I can't tell you where this happened, but it's a place with serious gopher issues. Despite the fact that the Rodenator is legal, effective, and even fun, my hosts were deeply concerned about backlash from vermin support groups.

I'm not. The Rodenator is every bit as cool as it sounds. Mounted on a small towed trailer, the contraption features twin tanks of propane and oxygen. Hoses from these tanks run into a long, evil looking nozzle.

When a burrow is located, the nozzle is plugged into the hole. Explosive gas in amounts ranging from "some" to "a whole bunch" is pumped into the ground. It filters silently through a warren of tunnels and dens.

Anyone home probably knows something is up. But just about the time they think, "Hey, what's that smell?" a trigger on the Rodenator is pulled and—BLAMMM!—their phone line chewing days are over.

The Rodenator crew I visited was good. Gary and Tolly were the gas passer and driver. Dino, Russ, and Oly showed me how to search a field for suspicious holes.

Gopher hole detection is two parts science, one part art, and maybe half a part thinking like a small, fidgety pest whose goal in life is to reach China.

A moderately energetic, non-union gopher will dig about ten billion feet of tunnel during its life, none of it straight or even logical. The only way to tell if a hole is promising is to dig out the front and stick your hand in it.

"This one looks good," Dino told me. His arm was in the ground up to his shoulder, his face a mask of concentration. "It splits three ways. One of them might be a dead end."

Dino got up. Gary placed the nozzle and stared at his watch. Everyone else backed up and stuck fingers in their ears. After 40 seconds, Gary shut the gas off and pulled the trigger.

Every Rodenator explosion is different. Sometimes it's just a sharp crack. Other times, say, if the gopher has a meth lab going, you'll hear it a mile away. But if the hole goes deep, there's just a satisfying thump and the ground jumps.

This time the detonation echoed off nearby buildings. Grass, dirt and gopher furniture flew in the air as the lawn unzipped in a line stretching 20 yards. Then it was on to the next hole.

I could have done this all morning. But the session only lasted two hours, and it wasn't covered by my insurance. I feel much better though.

SLT - July 20, 2009

NOTE: The secret location was actually the state prison at Point of the Mountain. For some reason management didn't want the public to know that they had a gopher problem requiring the use of explosives.

8   **Shocking Police Research**

Cops shot me with a Taser last week. I was minding my very own business when my entire body suddenly charley horsed and sparks came out of my behind.

I'd feel a lot better about the experience had I been robbing a bank, or punching a nun, or something. Unfortunately, I was only stupid. I asked for it.

The incident occurred during a Taser training class held at the Salt Lake County Sheriff's Office gun range. Cops from around Utah attended the class to learn how to become Taser instructors.

The Taser, of course, is the neuromuscular incapacitating device cops use to take less than cooperative people into custody. You've seen them on TV or in the news.

Neither my wife nor my editors wanted me to attend the class. I argued that someone in the news media needed to understand the Taser. They countered with, "You're fat. You're old. You'll die." I went anyway.

The X26 Taser looks like a gun that a clown would pull. It's a blunt, yellow, half-pistol contraption. It gets unfunny in a hurry though.

There isn't enough space here to describe the complete workings of the Taser. For more information, go on the Internet or a criminal rampage. Either way, you'll learn a lot.

Basically, a small nitrogen charge propels two barbed

darts into a suspect's body. Attached to the darts are wires along which passes an amount of electricity sufficient to cause a suspect to fall down and make noises like an aggrieved donkey.

The burst lasts five seconds or 350 years, depending on which end of the wires you're on. It's called "riding the five" by officers willing to submit to it for training purposes, and "What the [deleted] was that!?" by those who make the training necessary.

Before practicing with the Tasers, we learned some stuff about electricity, specifically the relative differences between volts, amperes, and something called joules, a French word meaning "Ouch!"

When it came time to ride the five, I was darted by the instructor, Arizona DPS Sgt. Bud Clark, whom I still respect as an instructor but no longer like as a person.

The darts struck me in the back and lower leg. The pain was immediate and intense, worse than anything I had ever felt before. My body became rigid and I made noises that still reverberate in space.

The pain ceased as soon as the electricity stopped flowing. Except for some minor befuddlement regarding why the hell I ever wanted to do such a thing in the first place, I was fine.

I have a new purpose in life. It's to live in such a way that the subject of the X26 Taser never comes up again.

SLT - October 23, 2006

9   **Fire On the Mountain**

South Mountain is the most prominent feature in my part of Herriman. It's the first thing I see every morning when I open the front door or the window blinds.

The mountain serves a number of important roles in my life. Its changing colors mark the passing of seasons. The steep draws and trails are where I hike to bird watch and get off by myself.

Best of all, South Mountain prevents artillery rounds from landing in my yard. Camp Williams is just on the other side. National Guard units preparing to deploy to Afghanistan use the firing ranges to tune up.

When I left church Sunday afternoon, I noticed a small yellowish plume rising behind South Mountain. I didn't think anything of it at first.

Within a couple of hours, the plume had swelled into a cloud of smoke that blotted out the sun. This was no ordinary blaze. The winds were driving something wicked our way.

As night fell, fire crested the mountain. It spilled toward our homes like lava, flames splashing down the draws and canyons. Word went out in the neighborhood to standby for possible evacuation.

Standby meant that my wife and I had plenty of time to think about what would fit into our vehicles. There were some tough choices, most divided along gender lines.

Huge TV or financial records? Wedding dress or back issues of Mad magazine. Good china or skeet thrower?

We were lucky. Standby gave us time to debate what was important to us. Other Herriman residents had only minutes to grab what they could before the flames were on them. Some were forced to leave virtually everything.

What would you take if you had just minutes to grab it? It's not a fair question. In reality it would be more like "What would you grab in one frantic trip through your house?

I would definitely take my wife. Without her, I probably couldn't keep a job. But assuming that she came along on her own, I would grab my computer, some photos, and a folder of documents.

By midnight, it was clear that we wouldn't have to leave. In many places, the fire was stopped within yards of homes. Others weren't so lucky. Morning light revealed burned out homes less than a mile from mine.

Some lost everything in what's been dubbed the Machine Gun Fire. We all lost something.

My loss is limited to the mountain itself. Opening my front door now reveals a hellish, seared landscape. The fall colors that marked winter's approach are gone, replaced by a coal dump.

The U.S. flag and staff at the top of the mountain have vanished. The old wooden crate I sat on to watch the sun rise when training for the Grand Canyon hike last year is probably cinders now.

I also lost friends. This morning I wondered if Hannity and Limbaugh, the two fat ground squirrels who yell at me whenever I pass, survived the blaze.

Spring runoff will bring the threat of erosion, but also the promise of new growth. Eventually—like the rest of us—

the mountain will bounce back. Until then, we learn to appreciate what we once took for granted.

SLT - September 21, 2010

10   **Restitution Solution**

First let me say that "machine gun fire" is a stupid name for a fire. It makes it sound like the Utah National Guard deliberately strafed Herriman instead of accidentally scorching it.

But the Guard is trying to make it right. A military claims center has been set up in Herriman City Hall to reimburse citizens for legitimate fire-related losses.

NOTE: The word "legitimate" is not intended to be misleading. People who think they're going to get money from the National Guard for every little expense—and there are more than a few—are in for a surprise.

I'm not one of them. My home was actually damaged. On the night of the fire, my wife and I watched helplessly as flames came within a mere, oh, thousand yards of our home. The following morning, our house smelled like Smoky the Bear's armpit.

Wednesday morning, I filed a claim for smoke damage. I gathered up all my documentation—a lone receipt for $2.67 —and drove over to City Hall. The place was hopping with soldiers and refugees.

As you might expect with the military, some paperwork was involved. Not a lot, but it made me nervous. The last time I did something like this, I ended up at Fort Jackson.

Once the form was completed (ten minutes tops), I sat

in a tent and played the military "hurry up and wait" game for what had to be almost an entire minute. Then I was ushered into the center for an individual interview.

I handed my file across a table to a soldier. He was a private, painfully polite and about ten years old. He photocopied my driver's license then examined my documentation.

PRIVATE: "This receipt is for…underarm deodorant?"

ME: "Yeah, I rubbed it on the walls and curtains. Some on Nu-Nu."

PRIVATE: "Nu-Nu?"

ME: "The dog. He smelled like smoke, too."

Asked if my deodorization method worked, I said the house smelled better but Nu-Nu wasn't a fan of Right Guard Fresh Blast. Also, my wife was mad about the curtains.

The private summoned a sergeant. The one who came over had at least a dozen stripes. This boded ill for my claim. I'm familiar with sergeants and stripes.

From prior experiences, I know that the more stripes a sergeant has the less he appreciates being bothered. Correspondingly, the greater the odds are that I'll end up being made to do something onerous lasting anywhere from a few minutes to "all *#@!% day!"

I don't even want to talk about officers. Unfortunately, I have to because that's where my claim ended up. After offering me some candy and apologizing for making me wait another entire minute, the sergeant showed me to a seat in front of a major.

The major looked at my file. He jotted a few notes and asked if I had been evacuated. I said no, that there was this television program I was watching. When he inquired about injuries, I showed him where Nu-Nu bit me.

My claim was denied. The major was very nice about it. He said underarm deodorant didn't fall within the Guard's parameters of compensation. I was then politely shown the door.

In the parking lot, I ran into an acquaintance in uniform. He told me not to feel too bad. The Guard was taking care of people, but it had also denied claims for thousands of dollars that were even more ridiculous than mine.

I'm OK. Counting the candy and the fact that I didn't have to do any pushups, I probably came out ahead.

SLT - October 2, 2010

NOTE: More than a year later, a U.S. Army captain working in the Pentagon called my house to inquire whether I was satisfied with the way my claim was handled by the military. I told them to use the money to buy another grenade or helmet.

11 The Legacy of Boom

Saturday night I sat on the front lawn with my family and watched as Herriman shot off fireworks from the rodeo grounds.

Herriman doesn't skimp when it closes out Fort Herriman Days. Detonations echoed off the mountains until the dog howled in the kitchen. The entire neighborhood was strobed in nuclear colors of crimson, bullion, emerald and cobalt.

From our yard we heard the mortars cough. Seconds later the sky would explode in a dazzling moment of creation. I like the big ones best. They tear open like a thought in the head of God.

We let my two-year-old granddaughter stay up. It was her first firework show. As the night tore apart overhead, she ran to each family member and pointed up. "Boo," she cried, awestruck. "Boo."

Boom. Damn right boom. Boom is the magic of life. And the show doesn't stop when the lights come on.

I tilted my head a few degrees to the north. In spite of the street lights and fireworks, I saw the tail of the Great Bear, Ursa Major. The Big Dipper reminded me that we are specks in the biggest firework of all.

Fifteen billion years ago, the Universe unzipped in an instant of pure light. It's still exploding. Countless galaxies like brilliant shrapnel race apart at incomprehensible speeds. Eventually, they say it will collapse back in on itself and die.

Explosions breed impatience, which in turn breeds a dangerous obliviousness. We rarely understand that we are fireworks in our own right—how we also sparkle, flash and die against the black screen of eternity.

Scattered on the lawn is a firework set in motion by my wife and me. In less than a blink of eternity our daughters have bloomed into dazzling explosions of their own. They've triggered secondary explosions. One just blazed past me in Elmo pajamas.

My own explosion, set in motion more than half a century ago, has reached its zenith and begun to fade. Soon it will sputter out altogether. Eventually, even those who witnessed its erratic rush will be gone.

We're too busy looking at our watches to realize that every second is its own burst of brilliant color. With the right tilt of your mind it's possible to see a 30 year career go by like a skyrocket, every punch of the clock a spark in a tail that's gone before you know it.

But we're a show in a show inside a show. Our trajectories are colored by the pinwheels and star shells and echoes of all the booms that went before us.

If we pay attention, maybe we'll be bright enough and loud enough to make the oohs and ahhs of those we love last long after we're gone.

SLT - July 2, 2008

12 Big Bottom Blues

Today, we are going to talk about our butts. It is an indelicate subject, but also a necessary one. Your butt may be trying to kill you.

Actually, we will talk about colon cancer. The colon is located right inside the behind. We cannot possibly discuss our colons while talking about our smiles.

So, butts it is. If you find the subject offensive: tough. This is a big newspaper paper. Read something else.

Colon cancer killed Bruce Hepworth, my best friend from high school. Two weeks ago, it latched onto my wife. You and I could have it right now and not even know it.

Do not let anyone tell you that Utah does not have a state lottery. About 5,000 Utahns will get colon cancer this year, and one of the unlucky winners could be you. Call it a crapshoot.

Whether or not you and I will get colon cancer depends on the odds, which increase according to age, weight and genetics. Irene's family has a history of colon cancer, which is why she scheduled a screening for herself.

Good thing, too. If she had let it go another year, we would probably be talking about her funeral plans right now instead of the quality of my help, specifically what kind of idiot washes a new pair of jeans in a load of whites?

Getting screened for colon cancer is not complicated.

Think using a garden hose to rid your lawn of a gopher. Basically, someone runs a really small camera inside your bottom for a quick peek.

What they look for in there are any signs that you may be developing a problem. Items of particular interest include polyps, lesions, tumors, ruptures, assorted litter, and dormant space creatures.

The human colon has about five turns in it, none of them banked for traffic going in this direction. So, there are plenty of places for stuff to hide. They almost missed my wife's tumor.

Also, not everyone is built the same. One of my friends has a digestive tract so rudimentary it belongs in a flatworm. You could screen Larry for colon cancer by shining a flashlight down his throat.

But since your colon is probably lots more complicated, you should seek the assistance of a professional, preferably someone whose business card does not contain the word "rooter."

There is a bright side. Just prior to the procedure, they render you completely unconscious. In fact, reading this column is probably more unpleasant than the actual procedure.

The most unpleasant part of a colonoscopy—aside from finding anything bad—is the preparation. The night before, you have to drink a purgative so powerful that you better be standing on a plastic drop cloth.

I had a colonoscopy several years ago. It wasn't the full screen, just a few turns and burns was all. I was awake for it. It was far more embarrassing than it was painful, which brings us to the real danger of colorectal cancer: human pride.

In the early stages, colorectal cancer is generally easy to treat. The problem is that people ignore the warning signs because having someone poke around in a place we don't even like to talk about is embarrassing.

Everyone has a butt, and they pretty much all operate the same way. You can't get away from yours, and pretending that it isn't there is just silly.

Do not let a stupid notion of maintaining your dignity kill you. Get screened, especially if you are over the age of 55, or related to someone who has had colorectal cancer.

Joking about the procedure may seem vulgar, but it's certainly easier to take than crying over a funeral.

SLT - April 11, 2002

NOTE: My wife narrowly survived colon cancer. She's been cancer free since 2003. We're still grateful to the Huntsman Cancer Institute for all their efforts.

13 Emergency Repair Kit

Following the recent disasters—hurricanes, war, Senate confirmations—I checked on the status of my family's emergency supplies.

Emergency preparedness was something I remember from Boy Scouts. Mostly I remember great personal emphasis being placed on running away whenever the emergency was caused by me.

Today, emergencies had to be managed rather than escaped. I distinctly remembered putting together some of those 72-hour emergency kits in two five-gallon buckets years ago. I found them in the basement.

In one bucket was a complimentary bar of motel soap, half a box of Cracker Jacks, a AA battery, a flashlight (two D batteries not included), two plastic sandwich bags, and a hat. The second bucket contained a nickel.

Obviously it's time to update. Conventional wisdom has held that a proper emergency kit contain everything you would need in order to survive roughly three days without assistance. Thanks to FEMA, we now know that it's more like a month.

At the very least, the kit should contain sufficient water, food, medicine, and items necessary to provide rudimentary shelter, light, and personal protection.

We don't have enough space to cover everything, but I wanted to point out some items absolutely essential to every

72-hour emergency kit, things without which society cannot endure for long.

DUCT TAPE: At least two rolls. It's a modern form of the all purpose animal skin. Duct tape can be used to build a shelter, patch clothes, rig snares, bind wounds and even tie up looters.

TOILET PAPER: Lots. You'll run out sooner than you expect. When that happens you really don't want the only other option to be duct tape.

CASH: At least a hundred bucks, some of it in singles and quarters. Sounds crazy, I know. But you never know when you might stumble across a working pay phone or vending machine. Also, you can use it to bribe looters.

PRESCRIPTION DRUGS: A bucketful of Lortab comes immediately to mind here. You may also want to consider the irony of surviving a disaster only to die a few days later for lack of whatever keeps you ticking now.

KEYS: Depending on the speed at which you are dying, not being able to drive your car, access the storage shed, or get into work following a big disaster can be hugely depressing.

KNIFE: Civilization is little more than the process of reducing ourselves to our most physically helpless level. It's amazing how we've allowed ourselves to be parted from this handiest of all human tools.

IDENTIFICATION: Granted, photocopies of drivers' licenses, birth certificates, and other official forms of ID won't help you survive a disaster, but they can make survival more enjoyable once/if the government shows up.

MONKEY: You have to let them out of the kit once in a while, but few things are more indispensable when lying pinned by rubble than being able to send a monkey for help.

GUN: If things get really bad, you can revert to the human ancestral means of providing for your family by shooting ducks and National Guard planes. Don't forget bullets.

CONTRACEPTIVES: Sex is a great emotional comfort, which is why calamities are always followed by an increased birth rate. Duct tape will work here, but you won't want it to.

SLT - October 3, 2005

14   Rules of the Road

Driving over Bruin Point in Carbon County last week, Sonny and I ran into bad weather. More accurately, it ran into us. We were there first.

In less than an hour we experienced rain, snow, hail, fog, lightning, thunder, and high wind. Following a 30 second intermission of sunlight, it started all over again.

The road was muddy, rutted, and boulder-strewn. Visibility wasn't too bad. At various times we could actually see through the mud on the windshield. Locked in low four-wheel drive, we kept climbing through the clouds.

Because I was driving, I made a conscious effort to stay in the ruts. It seemed the safest place to be even when we were rounding switchbacks sideways.

I could tell Sonny was nervous. He had slipped off his seat belt, placed both feet on the dashboard, and was keeping a hand on the door handle. He was in full ejection mode.

Bailing out of a moving vehicle isn't a good idea on relatively flat ground. But up on Bruin, you keep your options open. There are places so steep that you'll have another birthday before the mangled wreckage you're wearing comes to a complete stop.

Although Sonny and I have vastly different driving habits, it's a toss as to which of us is scarier behind the wheel. I get us into trouble by not paying attention. Sonny gets us there on purpose.

ME: "Um, you know that's a river, right?"

HIM: "Hold my Coke."

Over the years, Sonny and I have developed a system while driving some of Utah's worst byways, back roads that are in fact roads only through the application of serious imagination. But no matter how bad the roads get, the following rules have always brought us safely home.

RADIO CONTROL – No matter whose rig it is, the passenger controls the music. This is a form of self defense for the passenger. If you don't like how things are going outside, you can threaten the driver with some Neil Diamond inside.

The drawback is that if you don't change the CD or the channel, the driver may eventually drive off a cliff on purpose.

MIND YOUR HELM – Regardless of how aggrieved a passenger becomes by the view through the windshield, he is not allowed to wrest control of the wheel from the driver.

Conversely, the driver is expected to maintain physical control of the wheel at all times. This is less comforting than it sounds. I've seen Sonny steer with his teeth while cracking pistachios.

DEAD RECKONING – Although we rarely take them along, only the passenger is allowed to examine a road map while the vehicle is traveling at speeds in excess of 50 mph with two or more windows open.

ALL ABOARD – At no time may the driver deliberately abandon the passenger further than five miles from potable water, in a strange town at night, or within visual range of any predator larger (or quicker) than a turtle.

SILENT RUNNING – When stopped by law enforcement, only the driver is permitted to speak. We made this rule after I told a deputy sheriff that Sonny's inattentive driving was due to a mental condition.

When we got to the top of Bruin Point and had shoveled the mud and hail off the windshield, Sonny said we needed a new back road rule.

From now on, only the passenger is allowed to cover his eyes and scream.

SLT - October 18, 2010

15 **Garbage Sale**

Saturday is garage sale day. Also known as yard sales, estate settlements, rummage sales and crap-o-ramas, they generally amount to little more than paying a perfect stranger for the privilege of hauling their trash away.

But it is possible to find the occasional bargain cruising these sales. You can also ram your ride into the back end of some nitwit who stopped their car in the middle of the street to window shop at one.

Poor parking is a major yard sale risk. Most yards have less than a four-car frontage, not that this matters to bargain hunters who will gladly park on your roof if you let them.

On Saturday, I made it to the first yard sale without accident. My goal was to see how many I could get to in an hour (5). I was looking for a decent table saw and, if possible, a first edition "Moby Dick."

Everyone has heard the yard sale legends, tales along the lines of finding a Romanov broach or a Faberge egg in someone's junk jewelry bin and getting it for a buck.

Mostly it's just trash: romance novels, maimed Barbies, dingy clothing, barely used exercise equipment, bar fight furniture, chipped dishes and Cold War-era office machines.

Poking through someone else's junk is the perfect way to find out exactly who buys all that "what kind of an idiot would buy that?" stuff featured on late night TV infomercials.

I came really close to buying a crossbow, affordable at just $60. The seller was even willing to come down in price. Unfortunately, he wasn't also willing to come over to my house and take the beating I'd get for bringing it home.

A crossbow was not the only cool thing I dared not buy. There was a box of girlie magazines, one of those racist black jockey hitching posts, a pair of X-ray glasses with one lens missing, a dried bean and pea mosaic of either Elvis or Benito Juarez, and the entire LDS Journal of Discourses (minus volumes 2, 5, 6 and most of 9).

I made a generous offer on a live cat. Everyone needs a spare cat for research purposes. But the cat's owner refused to sell because, she said, "You're that guy from the Tribune."

For nine bucks I scored the following treasures: a gasoline nozzle complete with eight feet of hose, a whoopee cushion, corn on the cob butter dish, a large genuine vinyl not-a-hide handbag, a sprinkler toy in the shape of a circus seal, a 1979 Drug Reference, and a box of galvanized washers.

To fit in with the addled yard sale crowd, I plugged the gas nozzle into my car's tank and dragged the hose around as if I'd been in too much of a hurry to get there. Didn't even get a second look.

The only smart person I met all morning was a young gal on Morningstar Dr. She took the stuff her sister was going to throw away after cleaning out her room, and made $150 bucks in an hour by holding a yard sale.

I finally went to Sears and bought a table saw. Watch for it in my yard in another five years.

SLT - June 20, 2005

16 'Til We Beat Again

I descend through a long line of farm drudges. From harrowing fields in merry England to raising cricket fodder in Utah, my genealogy back to Abraham is a collection of subsistence farmers.

Tilling the soil should come naturally to me. It doesn't. My branch of the family tree was propelled from the land by a complicated agricultural process known as starvation. We became cops then a journalist.

But once a year I return to my familial roots. It happens every spring when my wife decides to spend 800 bucks to grow three tomatoes and a zucchini the size of a zeppelin.

We have developed a system for our type of gardening. I dig. She plants, waters, weeds, and harvests. It's fair. Digging is the hard part.

My ancestors used sticks, shovels and even their bare hands to turn the soil. I prefer things slightly less strenuous and would therefore use explosives if permitted. Instead, I use a motorized garden tiller.

My first tiller was a hand-me-down root-grabber of pre-war Czech origins that probably began life as a mine detector. Anyway, last year it coughed the spark-plug 500 feet into the air and stopped working.

I bought a new one. Today, I operate a new front-till 8-hp Rockfinder 500-Z with the optional pin striping and gopher decapitator. I'd drive it to church if the wife let me.

Things aren't easy even with a new power tiller. We live in Herriman where the ground is harder than the back of Dick Cheney's head. It's like tilling an airport runway.

The most important part of tilling is matching the right machine to the size of the garden. My wife's garden is so big that it's actually visible on a map of the world.

Garden tillers also come in various sizes, from the little macro jobs that barely manage to grub out a flower pot, to military-size machines with heavy armor and seating for a squad of laborers.

For all the advances in mechanized farming, the toughest part of turning the earth remains the same: Dogs. Really stupid dogs will try to bite the moving tines of a tiller. For a very short lived laugh, let them.

But right after that is rocks. No matter how soft the earth is God says it must contain a certain number of rocks. Where I live, that number is "all." A garden tiller lets you know when you've found one.

Churning along in whatever passes for dirt the tiller will suddenly begin hopping up and down. Eventually, it barfs out a rock that must then be lugged to a location from where it will crawl back to the garden during the night.

A tiller will dig up anything, including dog bones, pirate treasure, car parts, Mayan ruins, and stuff your wife says it wasn't supposed to. It's specialty, however, is yanking up sprinkler pipe.

The most memorable find this year was a rotting tarpaulin that wound itself around the tines in a knot the size of which can only be accurately measured with profanity.

For all their trouble, tillers are a blessing. Mostly it's a blessing that they weren't invented any earlier than they were.

My family might still be farmers.
   SLT - May 19, 2005

17 Training for the Olympics

Five days until the torch run. I get up every morning before dawn and drag myself over two miles of empty streets.

It's like an early scene from "Rocky," where Sly Stallone prepares to fight Apollo Creed---some guy thick of head and body training alone for a moment of glory. The big difference is that I'm not excited enough to drink raw eggs.

Training for the Olympics is tough. You have to prepare yourself mentally as well as physically. At least that is what I hear my fellow Olympians saying.

Zig von Oolonger (Biathlon) --- "Ze game ist all in zer head."

Komoloti Doh (Slalom) --- "Honorable effort shall my spirit to make."

Brad Jones (Snowboard) --- "Dude, it's whoa."

So, attitude is everything. Just getting me out of bed requires a lot of serious attitude. Right around the fourth time I hit the Snooze button, my wife puts both feet on my back and launches me across the room.

In every Olympic sport there is that supreme level of physical effort called "the wall," that point during training where it's do or die.

Punching through the wall is what separates contenders from pretenders. In the 0.02 mile torch run event, it's called "the porch." If I can just get off the %#@&! porch, I can probably make it the entire 350 yards.

Out on the cold, dark street I am alone with my thoughts. Can I go the distance? Do I have what it takes to be a champion? Are my shoes on the right feet?

Two blocks into the jog and I am ready to kill anyone who says it's all about attitude. Attitude doesn't keep your lungs from sticking out of your belly button. But I am improving. It's been a whole week since I called a cab.

I haven't yet reached the point where I sprint through downtown Salt Lake, and charge up the steps of the State Capitol. But I have reached that level of roadwork where I recognize all the dogs on my route.

When you're training for a major Olympic running event, dogs come in three categories. Bronze medal dogs stay in their yards and bark. Silver medal dogs snarl and come out for a sniff. Gold medal mutts will tear off your sweat pants if you don't outrun them.

Training doesn't end with road work. It continues back home where food is guarded by the training manager, in my case the same person who woke me up.

Diet is important. Real athletes must watch what they eat. This is to keep cheesecake and Snickers bars from cleverly disguising themselves as fruits and vegetables, which they always seem to do when you are training.

Thanks to a closely watched diet, I have managed to lose a total of two pounds. It's no coincidence that this is exactly how much a human liver weighs. If you found one on the road, there is a reward. Eventually, if you train the way you are supposed to, you begin to look like a champion. In the case of the torch run, this cannot be left to chance. So, they dress you.

I got my Official Torch Running Oufit™ in the mail

two weeks ago. White gloves, white beanie, white shirt, white pants, white windbreaker.

I tried it on. I looked like Liberace getting ready for bed.

The only apparel not provided were underwear and shoes. Being an iconoclast, I checked up on this. Maidenform is not an official Olympic sponsor. Neither is Tony Lama, a maker of fine cowboy boots.

Finally, there is the competition. You have to study those you plan to beat. Since the torch run is a solitary and non-timed event, and it's technically possible to "run" the torch on my hands and knees, I am completely optimistic.

Five days until we see if the training pays off. Five days until Grand Junction 2002.

SLT - January 29, 2002

NOTE: For all the training it was a relatively easy run for an old guy. It had a positive effect on my "Olympic outlook," which hadn't been exactly kind up to that point.

18 Checking Out the Other Side

I went to Relief Society last week. Although this wasn't a sin, I was supposed to be in High Priest Group where guys my age belong.

For you non-Mormons, Relief Society is the LDS church's organization for women. I happen to believe that it's the most important part. The church couldn't exist without it.

Some people think the priesthood is the most important part of our church. But I've been a Mormon my whole life and I know who does all the work.

Anyway, for some reason I decided that it was a complete waste of time to put on my good pants just for High Priests. I can stay home and listen to hound dogs snore.

(Here, I'll make it easy for you: *The Salt Lake Tribune*, 90 S. 400 West, Suite 700, SLC, 84101).

Even without the priesthood, the women of the Rosecrest First Ward caught on right away that something was amiss. I stood out like Wilford Brimley in a beauty pageant, a mule among deer.

It made them nervous. One or two women offered to show me to priesthood meeting. Several asked if I was lost, a rather pointless question considering to whom it was directed.

"Robert, what are you doing in here?" the bishop's wife finally demanded.

I said that I just wanted to see how the other half lived,

that I'd heard the lessons were grippers, and, more to the point, there might be snacks.

Actually, I said that Heavenly Father told me to be there. As explanations go this one is quite handy because they can't prove that He didn't.

I stayed for the entire bit. Here's my report:

Thanks to folding chairs, I come out of High Priests (when I do go) numb at both ends. Relief Society is the only classroom in a Mormon church where the chairs are padded.

It smells better. High Priests smells like Preparation H and dry scalp. But I'll bet half of any blessings I got coming that someone in Relief Society was wearing "White Shoulders."

The music is angelic. It helps that Relief Society had someone who played the piano. But it wouldn't matter if we had a band, priesthood bearers in the Rosecrest 1st Ward sing like oxen held at gunpoint.

The lesson was clearly prepared. By this I mean that some thought went into it, the teacher stayed on track, and no one—not even once—drew a corollary between the gospel of Jesus Christ and the NFL.

The downside? No snacks. Kids yodeled in the background. A bit formal. And unlike priesthood meeting, no one offered a counterpoint such as, "You're full of crap, Bill" to any part of the discussion.

It was good. I'll probably go back.

SLT - August 5, 2006

19   **Relief Society Application**

Last week I wrote about resigning my LDS church calling of eight years. I expected immediate contact from the bishop with another job offer, but it's been seven days and I'm still out of work.

It's not like I'm hard to find. The bishop lives right next door. He could call me to a new job over the fence. In fact, the last job he gave me was more of a yelling than a calling. Above the roar of a lawnmower, I was hollered to work in the Primary.

Since leaving on a mission, the longest I've ever gone without some kind of church calling is a month. It would have been a pleasant reprieve except that I was in Georgia and almost dead.

Maybe the reason I haven't heard from church leaders is because I offered to accept a calling as my ward's Relief Society president. And I'm a guy.

The Relief Society is the LDS Church's organization for women. As Mormon organizations go, it tends to be busier, more effective, and vastly more spiritual than any of the all-male priesthood quorums.

I've endured thousands of priesthood lessons, most of them every bit as enjoyable as having a hole scratched in my skull with a penny. Why wouldn't I rather be in Relief Society? If nothing else, it smells better.

While I haven't heard back from my local church

leaders about being Relief Society president, I have heard from readers. A lot.

The feedback was polarized between Mormon women who saw my offer to serve in the Relief Society as irreverent or even blasphemous, and Mormon women who said they would start attending church again if I was their president

SISTER A: "Your usual stupid comments. Who are you to say how the church operates?

SISTER B: "Please move to my ward."

Regardless of what you think, my proposal is certainly *au courant*. Some Mormon women are clamoring to be ordained. Seems fair that it should work the other way.

On the off chance that the stake president might still ask to see me, I should probably have a Relief Society presidential campaign platform and some idea of a Cabinet (counselors, secretary).

For starters, I would insist on equal representation on the podium every Sunday. I wouldn't necessarily want to sit with the bishopric, but it's only right that everyone be reminded which ward organization does most (if not all) of the work.

Next, there will be a diaper-changing room in the ward house staffed entirely by the priesthood. Those who actually want to be in church (women) will be able to drop off a malodorous child and have it cleaned and wrapped while they're busy elsewhere.

Homemaking meeting would make a comeback, only this time it would be for men. The Relief Society would teach priesthood holders lessons like "How To Load a Dishwasher," "Having A Meaningful Conversation," and "Making Dinner Your Own Damn Self."

As for who I would request as counselors, I would ask

the bishop for Sister—well, I'm not going to mention their names here. I'll only say that they're all capable, tough, and I'm a little afraid of them.

Finally, if I'm called as the Relief Society president, sisters in the Rosecrest First ward would be given permission to wear pants to church. Fair is fair. Their new president won't be wearing a dress.

SLT - November 2, 2013

20   Mormon Meany Matters

Shortly before leaving on my LDS mission in 1973, a coworker tried to get me to see the light by giving me the bloody details of the Mountain Meadows Massacre.

In 1857 an immigrant wagon train was slaughtered near Cedar City. The actual perpetrators of the massacre had long been debated, but the truth was finally coming out. Jordan was extra happy about that.

JORDAN: "And it was the Mormons who killed them."

ME: "Yeah, I know. Two of my great-great-grandfathers helped."

The fact that I already knew what had happened and was related to some of the murderers didn't sit well with Jordan. How could I possibly still go on a mission knowing that stuff about the church?

That part was easy--it had nothing to do with me.

While troubling, Mountain Meadows didn't surprise me. I already knew a few Mormons so steeped in church obedience that with the right prompting they'd probably do it again. As I saw it, my whole job was to make sure that I wasn't one of them.

Ditto polygamy, blacks and the priesthood, and a bunch of other troublesome stuff in our past. I've always believed that people are bad, including (and sometimes especially) people who are trying to be good.

I bring this up because in a recent address to a group of historians, Pres. Dieter F. Uchtdorf, second counselor in the LDS First Presidency, encouraged Mormons to maintain hope in the face of troubling explanations.

When the Tribune reported on it, I started getting feedback from readers eager to prove to me that the church I attend isn't "true" because our history proves it.

EMAIL: "The shame alone should tell you what you need to do, Mr. Kirby. Get out now."

ME: "OK, let me think ab...no."

I'm Mormon. It's who I am. Yeah, there are things I don't like about my church, but there are things that I do.

It helps that I'm comfortable being my kind of Mormon. It helps me handle people who think they have a better idea what I should do than me.

When I read the story about Pres. Uchtdorf's remarks, my first thought was who better than him to give such advice?

Pres. Uchtdorf belongs to a group of people with a dark and horrible past. And it isn't Mormons. He's German. He's probably spent his entire life hearing about the Holocaust, genocide on an industrial scale.

So even though he's now a naturalized U.S. citizen, I wonder why he didn't renounce his German heritage? He doesn't have to be German.

More to the point, why would a guy descended from such horribleness actually volunteer to serve in the *Bundeswehr* (post-war German army)?

Even though we belong to same church, Pres. Uchtdorf and I don't exactly travel in the same circles, so I have to guess about this. I'd guess that he's proud of being German and having served as a fighter pilot in the West German Air Force.

Should he hang his head in shame? Or does he tell

himself--rightly so--that what Germans did a long time ago doesn't change the kind of person he is today. And maybe that sticking around was the best thing for him to do.

Makes sense to me. I don't want to be something else. I'm comfortable being where I am.

That doesn't sit well with people both in the church and out who arrogantly presume to tell me what I should do. Fortunately for me, the answer is the same for both groups. All else aside, I'd probably stay Mormon just to piss you off.

SLT - March 15, 2014

NOTE: One of the things I still marvel at after 20 years is the constant rancorous debate between Mormons, non-Mormon, ex-Mormons, and jack Mormons. A column on rush hour gridlock will, within half a dozen reader responses, spin into a dogfight about polygamy and blood atonement.

21   **Getting Into Conference**

Thousands of Mormons are flocking to the church's 176th Semi-annual General Conference this morning, jostling for parking and seating and family connections. It can get a little crazy.

After every conference, hundreds of small children and the elderly—who failed to understand exactly which planter or lamppost "we'll all meet by"—are rounded up and sent as forced labor to Welfare Square.

I made that up, of course. The truth is that post-Conference strays are summarily shot by church security and then run through the Temple Ready program just to be safe.

Here, give my editor an earful at unchristlikeresponse @tribune.yel

The morning press into the Conference Center is the gauntlet Mormons run twice a year in order to get the gospel straight from our leaders' mouths—and to hear what a damnable bunch we are from the Insult for Jesus crowd.

Although it may seem like every Mormon in the entire world is trying to cram his or herself into the Conference Center, most of us won't get anywhere near the place.

The Conference Center is huge. You could hold blimp races in it. But it still isn't big enough to hold all Mormons. It isn't even big enough to hold all the Mormons who show up.

Most Mormons will attend Conference in the spirit,

which is to say electronically. Our attendance today and tomorrow will be courtesy of the wonderful miracle of mass media technology, which we recognize as a vile polluter of the human soul the rest of the year.

A Mormon my entire life, I have attended General Conference in the flesh less than a dozen times. Not because I don't think Conference is important, but because for much of my life I didn't live anywhere near Utah.

During that time, I got Conferenced via word-of-mouth, church magazines, radio and TV. These contain all of the rich Conferency goodness without any of the mood-altering scramble for parking.

After we moved to Utah, I caught the real thing a few times. It was nice, including the April Conference I got stung by a bee because the Tabernacle was full and I had to sit outside. But I went back to televised Conference.

The nice thing about televised Conference is I can argue with the speakers and not have to worry about getting dragged off by security.

I also prefer hearing "we are living in the last days" with my arm around a bag of Doritos. I don't like hearing it with someone else's breath on the back of my neck and the nagging suspicion that my car is being towed.

If you're going to Conference tomorrow, you can have my spot. I'll watch for you on television. Don't forget to wave.

SLT - September 30, 2006

22 **Street Screeching**

This is my 174th Semiannual LDS General Conference report. Exactly how much of it was prompted by the Spirit is easy. None.

I tried to keep the Spirit. In an effort to avoid last conference's brief bout of parking related atheism, I rode TRAX to Temple Square. My motive was pure, but it was still fraught with risk.

Two hours early on Saturday, white shirts and ties still crammed every TRAX stop. UTA put on extra trains. More sorely needed were additional ticket machines. Conference goers bunched around them in wide-eyed confusion.

You have to appreciate the irony of a people who profess to understand what God expects of them, yet are so easily baffled by ticket machines. English, Spanish, Braille, prayer; none of it helped. Trains came and went while we waited for them to figure it out.

Eventually those experienced with modern idolatry started reaching over timid shoulders and pushing the correct buttons for them. I can only hope they will return the favor at the Pearly Gates.

Forty minutes later, I got off at the Temple Square stop along with every other Mormon in the world. We thronged and mobbed and packed our way toward salvation with the same paradoxical behavior we live our lives.

Where harried cops directed traffic, faithful crowds obediently waited to cross streets. Absent authority the mob jaywalked with abandon. They darted ahead of trains and through traffic, blithely ignoring horns and the interdenominational gesture of impatience from drivers.

Authority around Temple Square was both real and imagined. The street screamers were out in force with their usual Hitler-at-Nuremburg pronouncement of God's merciless love. They bellowed and waved signs and did whatever it took to get noticed by Mormons and, more importantly, the media.

One saw me taking notes and came over to comment for the record about "Mr. and Mrs. Hinckley and all Mormons" eventually burning in the fiery pit.

I shrugged. "Then maybe we should just give them credit for behaving themselves before it happens."

"The Word says I cannot," he shouted, waving a ratty-looking Bible at Satan's well-dressed minions. "They are already DAMNED!"

"Well, be careful then. If they ever start believing you, there'd really be no reason for them NOT to kick your ass."

Miffed, he moved off looking for someone with a less flexible view of The Word. You just can't talk religion with some people.

Not all Mormons suffered in silence. One or two lost their bead on love and shouted back. Most simply ignored their critics and hurried inside to vote unanimously on two new apostles.

Conversely, not all non-Mormons were jerks. "Standing Together," an evangelical Christian group—"sugar-coated or pansy Christians" to the street screechers—showed up to wish Mormons a Happy Conference.

Eventually, I had to leave the show outside for the one

inside. But as usual when I got to the door of the Conference Center, I didn't have a ticket. Worse, there were no machines selling them.

It's the story of my spiritual life. I rode an empty TRAX car back home and watched Conference on television where I belong. In my own personal hell, at least there is diet Coke.

SLT - October 4, 2004

23   Should Have Been a Cowboy

TAVAPUTS RANCH – My wants are simple. In a freezing wind and atop the world's dumbest horse, I'd still rather be a lowly ranch hand on Tavaputs plateau than the mayor of New York City.

On Monday, I was. My friend Mark Connolly and I signed up as day drovers for Tavaputs Ranch, an aspen and sage covered spread the size of Rhode Island that overlooks Desolation Canyon of the Green River. There is no more beautiful place in the world.

It was the beginning of the ranch's fall cattle drive, when cows are gathered into a herd and "punched" down the canyon to their winter range near Price.

NOTE: No one really knows where the term "punching" cows originated. Linguists generally agree that it was in the American West and involved equal parts frustration and alcohol.

I can certainly understand why someone would want to punch a cow. A single bovine on a good day is irascible and easily spooked. Fifty of them with year-old calves are only slightly more reasonable than a federal agency.

After a huge breakfast, ranch owner Butch Jensen led us out to the corral. The day's crew consisted of half a dozen drovers of varying experience, an equal number of horses, and a mob of dogs.

Butch's son, Tate, asked what kind of mount I preferred. When I said, "one with power steering," he picked an enormous black...thing. Tate assured me that it was a horse, but it looked more like God had changed his mind in the middle of making a giraffe.

The horse's name was Stimulus. Butch said it was because they got him from a banker. As horse names go, it was better than Spine Cracker, Thunderbolt, or Menopause. Still, I suspected some form of low cowboy humor in the works.

Among the spur and bit crowd, there is no finer form of entertainment than watching a bi-polar horse pitch a fat tourist into a hospital bed.

Fortunately, the name fit. Throughout the day, Stimulus's contribution to the job at hand was tardy, erratic, and of dubious benefit. At one point, he simply stopped moving. Nothing I did—yelling, booting, pleading—had any effect.

As the rest of the drovers disappeared down a sunlit draw, Stimulus braced himself, stretched his neck, and whinnied at the other horses. It sounded like Bette Midler being electrocuted.

One of the real cowboys came back and took the reins from me. He said Stimulus was normally used for trail rides and this was the turnaround point. Being a union horse, Stimulus figured it was quitting time.

Towed along like a packhorse, we caught up with the rest of the group. It was embarrassing but helped reformat Stimulus's head. He followed the other horses as we began hunting cows.

Range cows are not like regular cows. In addition to being more independent, they've just spent an entire summer raising calves among cougars, coyotes, snakes and lightning.

Consequently, they're not of a mind to take any crap off a bunch of *#&@! cowboys.

The idea was to comb the draws and hollows, pushing the cows toward a collection point where a larger herd would be formed.

Watching a real cowhand and horse work together is a marvel. They seemed fused into one creature. Tate and his horse knew exactly what to do in order to get two dozen cows headed in the right direction.

I didn't and neither did Stimulus. His contribution to the gather largely consisted of staring off in some other direction, going to the bathroom, and occasionally trying to rub me off on a tree.

Hours later, Butch, Tate, and the real cowboys had a huge crowd of cows mooing their way in the right direction. It sounded like church.

I am not a natural rider. I suspect Stimulus understood this. He altered his gait in such a way that I might as well have spent the day hopping up and down on top of a fence post.

Somewhere at the tail end of the herd and the day, Stimulus and I reached an understanding. If I would stop cursing directly into his ear, he would quit trying to bite my leg. In the cold, bright afternoon, we rode drag, which, trust me, doesn't mean the same thing on a cattle ranch as it does in a New York nightclub.

SLT - October 7, 2009

24   **Learning and Loss**

I got to know Tate Jensen in a hail storm two years ago. We were pushing a herd of cows into Range Creek when the sky suddenly went dark.

What started out as a flurry of ice pellets soon graduated into an avalanche of ball bearings. Everyone scrambled for rain slickers.

There's very little shelter in Range Creek and none on top of a horse. But we had a herd to move. We kept riding while the hail grew in size, tenderizing us and 400 cows.

I do not suffer in silence. Yeah, suffering is an inescapable part of life. I get that. But when suffering involves me, I refuse to keep quiet about it.

Riding along in the slop of mud, manure, ice and torn leaves, I complained at length about cows, the weather, and the grudge Mother Nature seemed to bear us.

Tate looked over at me. On his wet face was the same easy-going expression he wore when the sun was shining on it 10 minutes ago.

"It can't last forever," he said.

He had a point. I'd never seen weather that lasted forever. Five minutes later the sun was out.

It was the first of many things I learned while pushing cows with Tate, including:

- Never feed another man's working dog.

- You'll always lose a fight with a mule.
- Bear poop is a good sign that it's time to go the hell somewhere else.

But it was Tate's common sense observation about the weather that stuck with me. Some things simply cannot be reasoned with, so don't bother.

From a life spent in the open, Tate had learned what some people never do—that everything in life is temporary. And when you have no say about it, the only thing you can do is put your head down and ride it out.

I spent a lot of time thinking about that. Human beings have a tendency to live entirely in the moment. That's why misery seems like it will last forever. So too do the things that we take for granted. But nothing in this life lasts, including us.

On Sunday night, Tate was murdered at his home in Price. The details are still sketchy, but the easy going cowboy I knew was shot to death over something so ridiculous that it will probably never be fully comprehended.

My own grief is barely tolerable. It pales in comparison to what Tate's family has to endure. The mere thought of what his parents Butch and Jeanie are going through is almost more than I can stand.

In a few days, Tate will be laid to rest on the high plateau he loved. Meanwhile, life hasn't stopped for the rest of us. There's still a herd to move, a ranch to winterize, and a thousand other things that need doing despite the emotional weather.

Grief can't last forever, either. The paralyzing sorrow will lessen over time, becoming more manageable. Eventually, the storm will lift a bit and we'll be able to smile again when we miss him. Until then, we keep moving.

Tate Jensen. 1980-2011. Ride out.

SLT - September 3, 2011

NOTE: Easily one of the toughest columns I've ever written.

25 Tavaputs Plateau Oysters

Sonny and I spent the weekend at Tavaputs Ranch. Located hell and gone east of Price, it's our favorite place to go be ourselves.

The ranch is owned by Butch and Jeanie Jensen. Sonny and I like Jeanie. She's one of only three women in the entire state who can stand the two of us together for longer than a minute without bursting into tears.

In turn, we fix things for her. Actually, Sonny fixes them. I chase tools for him. On Saturday, we repaired two doors, some shelves, a window, a bathroom, a rock wall, and an outhouse.

This particular trip to Tavaputs stood out for a couple of reasons. First is that neither of us was seriously injured by an animal.

NOTE: I did fall (or was pushed) off a small cliff. I'm OK now except for a persistent numbness in my feet.

Second—and far more potentially disconcerting—is that we ate Rocky Mountain oysters for the first time.

I should point out here that Tavaputs ranch grub is always delicious. It's the only place I work that hard and still gain weight. I once ate a steak there the size of a crib mattress.

Sunday morning was no different. Breakfast was fresh trout, watermelon, scrambled eggs, and, of course, the aforementioned oysters.

There's really no way to describe this politely, so I'm just going to say it. Rocky Mountain oysters are the, um, eye-watering parts of what was once a boy cow.

The "oysters" are harvested during the spring drive, when the boy cows become "steer" cows through a process known as castration.

I've been on these drives. The oyster gathering is almost always done by the women, who, frankly, rather seem to enjoy it. The cowboys (including me) stay safely in the saddle and try not to whimper in sympathy.

Once gathered, the oysters are taken back to the ranch and refrigerated until they can be served to ranch guests.

On Sunday, the guests were Sonny, me, assorted tourists preparing to depart on a river trip, and the ranch hands. The oysters were battered, seasoned, and pan fried. In appearance, they resembled nothing so much as deep fried marbles.

The ranch hands wolfed down the oysters as if they were nothing unusual, which they probably weren't. The tourists who were daring enough, gagged down one or two and even managed a weak smile.

Sonny and I ate half a dozen each. The texture was about what you'd expect from a kidney or a gizzard, and were, in the main, delicious.

When breakfast was over, Jeanie asked Sonny and I if the "oysters" tasted anything like we imagined they would.

After a bit of nervous dissembling, we confessed that regular guys like us don't spend a lot of time wondering what testicles taste like, so we had no real preconceived expectations.

Later, when Sonny and I were shoulder deep fixing an outhouse, he asked what I thought of Rocky Mountain oysters.

"Let's just forget about it and keep working," I said. "I don't want to make Jeanie mad."

SLT - August 3, 2011

26 Going Greek in Utah

The Greeks invaded Utah in the late 1800s. So many of them came here to work in the mines that the local copper pit came dangerously close to being renamed Kennecottakis.

NOTE: Most Utah historians won't agree with me about that, perhaps because I just made it up. It is true that a lot of Greeks came here though.

It's a good thing, too. Absent any other group to malign in appreciable numbers—Greeks got blamed for everything in Utah. This is particularly true during the early 1900s.

Back then, if a newspaper headline announced a wounded police officer, a bootlegging operation, or a fire of suspicious origin, the account always seemed to end with "a number of Greeks were seen leaving the area."

Outside of Mormons, no other group in Utah took care of its own better than the Greeks. If you were Greek and showed up here at loose ends, other Greeks took you in, fed you, found you a job, and made sure you behaved yourself within the norms of a highly passionate culture.

I have a copy of the 1892-1920 mug shot book for the Salt Lake City Police Department. Among the over 2,000 entries, there isn't one of a Greek man being arrested for vagrancy, begging, or even aggravated mopery. And there are no Greek women arrested for prostitution.

What Greeks got arrested for back then was attempted

murder, actual murder (typically of other Greeks), and large-scale bootlegging. Work or play the Greeks did not mess around, folks.

Hard working, family oriented, and a little crazy: that's my kind of people.

I figured it would be worth driving all the way to Carbon County on Friday just for lunch. The annual Greek Festival was in full swing when I arrived at Assumption Church in Price.

A lunch line (mostly non-Greeks) and barbecue smoke was wrapped around the church. My wife and I located friends Butch and Jeanie and tried not to drown in our own saliva while we waited.

It was worth the wait. In addition to a strong work ethic, lots of kids, and volatile temperaments, the Greeks also brought decent cooking to Utah.

When my Mormon pioneer ancestors arrived here, they considered roots and berries fine cuisine. Years later we were still eating a porridge called "lumpy dick."

When the Greeks came, they brought tyropitas, saganaki, gyros, and dolmades. Any fool can cook, but it takes thousands of years of real culture to turn a feast into an art form. I ate tyropitas (cheese pastry) until I cried. And then I ate some more.

After lunch, we took a tour of Assumption Church. We watched dancers and we talked with some local Greek families.

As we were leaving, someone suggested that for a true Greek cultural experience I needed to try ouzo, an aperitif of which Greeks are enormously proud.

I declined. Some things you can't fool me twice about. Ouzo tastes like someone boiled the Easter Bunny in jet fuel. Too much will give you a licorice-flavored hangover that lasts the better part of a week.

For over a hundred years now, Greeks have added color and taste to the history of Utah. Boy, did this place need them.

SLT - July 12, 2010

27 Suiting Up for the Devil

Last Sunday, a talk in Sacrament meeting was about putting on the armor of God, an equipment check of the spiritual battle gear needed to bang heads with Satan.

According to the speaker, emerging victorious from such a battle required a shield of prayer, a sword of faith, a helmet of scripture study, and a breastplate of…whatever.

I don't remember. I've heard this battle-ready analogy a lot over the years. The weapons always change according to the needs of the lesson. It was probably the breastplate of Family Home Evening.

Truthfully, shield, sword, and helmet aren't a lot of protection. That's all the Spartans had in "The 300," and they got the stuffing kicked out of them. So will you. The Devil's tough and he has his own gear.

From personal experience, I can tell you that Lucifer is very handy with the slingshot of sloth, the dagger of indifference, and the catapult of not getting your home teaching done.

Write this down. It's a list of spiritual gear that speakers and instructors never mention but are of paramount importance based on what gets stressed at church.

For example, did you plan on kicking Satan's ass barefoot? I didn't think so. For that job you'll need the steel toe boots of correlation.

One of Satan's favorite moves is the low blow of pornography. A helmet isn't going to do you a bit of good there. You'll need the athletic cup of chastity. Do not do battle in cyberspace without it.

An item that no one thinks about until it's too late is the mouth guard of reverence. You do not want to show up at the Judgment Bar without any spiritual front teeth. Heavenly Father will ask what happened to them.

The Devil doesn't always have to use a weapon. Sometimes he'll just stick a finger in your eye. Make sure to don your safety spectacles of the straight and narrow way.

As far as weapons go, I'm not a big sword of faith guy. I prefer the hatchet of hope or even just the lighter mallet of cooperation.

Some people like to load up on the armor. They'll don breastplates of convention that would stop a javelin of original thought from a dozen yards.

Unfortunately, all that armor will slow you down and won't do you a bit of good if one of Satan's elephants of light mindedness sits on you.

Let's not forget germ warfare. After a battle, you can't just track Satan's guts all over Heaven. Clean up with the Sani-Wipes of pure thought.

I hope this helps. If you're not into doing battle with Satan, and prefer to negotiate instead, keep the derringer of deathbed repentance handy.

SLT - February 2, 2008

28   Zion Trek Fashions

I'm somewhere in Wyoming dressed in realistic Mormon pioneer garb: hat, suspenders, shirt, clodhoppers, and a layer of sweat.

Dressing like a pioneer was one of the prerequisites for tagging along with Sandy Canyon View Stake on their Mormon handcart trek reenactment. The dress code for wandering aimlessly in the desert turned out to be stricter than the one for sitting in church.

We were given a list of forbidden trek fashions: no blue jeans, baseball caps, Grateful Dead T-shirts, bikinis, parachute pants, surfer shorts, etc. Participants were asked to carefully attire themselves in the manner of their stalwart ancestors.

A certain amount of realism is important in any reenactment. If pioneer dress was called for, I would strive to give them exactly that.

I shopped around for a granny dress, bonnet, apron and brogans, but none in my size could be found. Apparently even your really stalwart Mormon pioneer women weren't as stalwart as me.

Most illustrations of pioneers show guys sporting enough facial hair to stuff mattresses, so I tried growing a beard. After two weeks I looked like a badly radiated gorilla. I shaved it off but kept the usual mustache. My upper lip hasn't seen sunlight in 30 years.

Rounding up the necessary clothing took some work. I don't have suspenders or pioneer shirts just hanging in my closet. The furthest back my wardrobe extends is disco.

Fortunately, there was plenty of advice. Once word got out that I was going on the trek, tips from past trekkers poured in. They directed me to western clothing stores, Deseret Industries, military surplus outlets, and even Dumpsters.

I found a hat immediately. It looks very pioneer-ish. Unfortunately, it's also 100 percent wool. I wore it on a long afternoon walk last week. It certainly blocked the sun but kept me no cooler than if someone had sewn a brim around a yak.

Shirt and trousers were easy. I found them in a second-hand store. The shirt previously belonged to a member of a mariachi band, but it was OK once I cut the sequins off. The pants appear to be ex-Ukrainian army issue.

I also heard from historical purists, or people commonly referred to as "deranged." One told me that I should avoid any clothing with snaps, zippers, plastic buttons, Velcro, and collars. None of these items were invented in 1856.

Another historical anal-yst said I wouldn't get the full trek experience unless I treated the reenactment as a "reexactment."

When asked about the Dr. Scholl's Massaging Gel inserts I planned to put in my boots, his response was a scathing list of things the Mormon pioneers did without in order to cross the plains—air mattresses, foot powder, Pepto-Bismol, sun screen, insect repellant, etc.

Know what else the Mormon pioneers did without while crossing the plains? Temperance. The Word of Wisdom didn't become serious LDS church policy until long after Zion was settled.

So, if I couldn't bring Dr. Scholl along because he

wasn't historically accurate, I was bringing Captain Morgan and Jose Cuervo.

Fortunately, the people in charge of this trek have much better hats. Cooler heads pointed out that the trek experience is supposed to be faithful to history within reason.

I wish they told me that before I cut the zipper out of these pants.

SLT - July 30, 2008

29   Church in the Mean Time

From my front porch I can hit with a rock roughly half the people I see at church on Sunday. Wait a few minutes and the other half will drive by and I can get them too.

Being a go-to-church Mormon in Utah means living so close to fellow ward members that not much happens the entire congregation doesn't know about in five minutes.

If you get promoted, arrested, pregnant, fired, or just locked out of the house in your underwear, it's general ward knowledge almost before it stops happening.

Religion normally doesn't get this nosy outside of an armed compound. This kind of cheek-to-jowl living can be intrusive and is considered by some as one of the biggest drawbacks to active participation in Utah Mormonism.

It also happens to be one of our greatest strengths. You just have to wade through a lot of church to appreciate it.

At work on Tuesday, I caught the noon news broadcast on television. A van had been obliterated in a traffic crash. A young mother and two small children were being rushed to emergency rooms by helicopter and ambulance.

I tuned it out. Not my job. None of my business.

Hours later I learned that the van belonged to the young couple living across the street from me in Herriman, Eric and Jeana Quigley.

Not only do I see the Quigleys in church, I actually

have hit Eric with a rock. We ate dinner with them at a neighborhood party the night before the crash. Our grandkids played with daughters Bianca and Miranda.

The accident occurred as Jeana took her daughters to swimming lessons. While making a turn in an intersection, their van was struck broadside by a truck. The impact spun them into the path of another vehicle that also slammed into them.

Jeana was knocked unconscious and badly lacerated. Aside from assorted bruises, 4-year-old Bianca's most significant injury was the outrage she felt when paramedics cut off her new swimming suit.

Fourteen-month-old Miranda suffered serious head injures and died three days later at Primary Children's Hospital.

Here's where all that nosiness and boring church pays off.

Although the accident occurred several miles from home, the dust literally had not settled before someone from the ward stopped and was pulling through the wreckage. The rest of the ward knew about it before the cops and paramedics showed up.

Ward members went to all three hospitals, contacted Eric at work, and organized into labor squads. People who didn't get in on the immediate need level were frantic for some way to help.

In 48 hours, the Quigley yard was mowed, home cleaned, laundry done, refrigerator stocked, relatives fed, and a trust fund set up at a local bank. We would have given their dog a bath if they had one.

There's a positive side to the congregational microscope my ward lives under, one shared to varying degrees by those in other churches. What happens to a few happens to all.

Today, I cut church some slack. Today I say the point of all that nosiness is to wind us up for moments like this, times when we won't tune it out because it is our job and our business.

SLT - July 30, 2005

30   Sage Advice Rebellion

I try not to lend my support to causes, even good ones. Bitter experience has taught me that there's no cause or organized purpose so important that it needs the help of yet another imbecile.

But occasionally I'm forced into a cause through no fault of my own. This particular one is the Sagebrush Rebellion.

Until last week, I thought the Sagebrush Rebellion was a guerilla operation conducted by a radical species of desert plant attempting to throw off the shackles of oppression through suicide sneezing.

It's not. *Artemisia tridentata* is the Latin name for sagebrush. I didn't know that either. I looked it up on the Internet, which immediately gave me the option of clicking on "sagebrush" or "Italian porn star."

Eight hours later I understood that the Sagebrush Rebellion is in fact a concerted effort by Western ranchers to shoot at federal workers over something patriotic. It's complicated.

My understanding increased a hundredfold when a SWAT team from the Bureau of Land Management raided my home on Monday. With a jackboot on my neck, they accused me of supplying heavy weapons to the Sagebrush Rebellion.

BLM Guy: "Do you deny that, Mr. Kirby?"

ME: "You got the wrong guy. My name is Art Tridentata."

This column would be a lot more interesting if any part of that incident were true. What actually happened is a lot less exciting.

A nice woman from the BLM called and violated my rights by asking if I had killed anyone or anything with a bowling ball?

Permitted to contact my attorney, I would have only said through him, "Not recently." However, denied legal counsel, the best I could come up with at the time was, "Umm..."

After the initial confusion (all of it mine) the BLM lady said the agency was simply addressing public concerns about a recent column that had me scaring some cows with a bowling ball cannon.

For the record, it was Sonny's idea. I tried to stop him but it was too late. The cannon had gone off and the cows were already badly frightened. They were last observed in a high speed turn around the corner of a mountain toward Nevada.

The BLM lady said we hadn't done anything illegal, but cautioned us to shoot our cannons in such a manner that we didn't hit--intentionally or otherwise--someone else using public land.

Finally, it was suggested we might perhaps clean up after ourselves. Surely even a newspaper columnist understood that it's ecologically unsound to leave bowling balls in the desert.

I agreed. A half buried bowling ball loitering in the shade of some sagebrush can easily be mistaken by a passing desert tortoise as a possible date.

There's no worry about us abandoning bowling balls in

the desert. They're hard to come by. Not only are they nearly impossible to shoplift, most gun stores don't even sell them. So we never just leave them in the desert or someone's roof.

The good news is that we're not the only ones shooting bowling balls. The last time we shot, we took 10 bowling balls and came home with 12.

We killed a lot of sagebrush though, so I wouldn't worry too much about the rebellion.

SLT - April 22, 2014

31   **Church Snacking**

A couple of years ago, one of the children in my LDS ward asked me an important gospel question. It was Fast Sunday and Tanner had been watching me eat M&M's during Sacrament meeting.

TANNER: "Brother Kirby, are you bad?"

ME: "Oh, yeah. Ask the bishop."

I told Tanner that I was trying to be better, but I had been forced to move to his neighborhood after being kicked out of my last ward because I ate a Primary kid.

Wide-eyed, Tanner accepted the claim as fact. He nervously asked, "All of him?"

I confessed that I hadn't eaten the kid's elbows because there wasn't a lot of nutritional value in them. Tanner mulled this over in his troubled four-year-old brain.

TANNER: "Was he yucky?"

ME: "Like monkey, only stringier."

Tanner scooted closer to his mom. Bad as this sounds I think the imagery of me eating a kid really helped him put Fast Sunday M&M's into the proper perspective.

Being a Mormon means I can pretty much eat whatever I want. We have few solid dietary restrictions (and it shows), including anything specific on cannibalism.

Granted, it would be a sin to kill someone just for lunch, but there's nothing in any temple recommend interview I ever sat through that specifically says we can't eat somebody who is already dead.

Other faiths aren't quite so lucky. Banned or discouraged foods in these groups range from snakes to pigs to mules and even iguanas. I've never had filet of mule, but it sounds perfectly awful.

Depending on the particular faith and one's level of commitment, interpreting these dietary restrictions can be complicated. Muslims, for example, are permitted by the Quran to eat chickens on the one hand, but forbidden on the other to eat "animals without ears."

Since chickens have no discernible ears, I'm not sure how they figure this one out. If it's anything like where I go to church, it probably generates more than a few pointless arguments.

Mormons like to bicker about caffeine. We're not supposed to drink coffee or tea, and cola soda drinks are strongly discouraged.

Exactly how much caffeine it takes to make a beverage illegal is still a matter of much debate. The only thing we get sillier about is movie ratings.

It makes sense to eat healthier. It can even be argued that eating right enables one to feel better and perhaps then even more spiritual. I don't know, I've never tried it.

I don't plan on it, either. Basing my diet on Hostess products doesn't make a lot of sense, but I'm not sure a Biblical diet would put me in a more spiritual frame of mind.

If all I had for breakfast were an ounce of millet husks, a locust, and a dab of honeycomb, chances are I'd be pretty irritable. I'd definitely eat a kid then.

After church, Tanner came over to clarify things. He had asked his mom about it, and she had set the record straight.

TANNER: "You can't eat kids."

ME: "Sure you can. But you have to fatten them up first. Want some M&M's?"

SLT - January 8, 2011

32 **And I'm a Mormon...**

You've seen the TV commercials. Someone will come on the screen and tell you all about how they're just a regular person: "I'm a mother, a doctor, a homemaker."

Then comes the kicker: "And I'm a Mormon."

Some of these people were intended to be surprises but actually weren't: black people, Asians, Hispanics, maybe an Egyptian, or even an Eskimo.

I haven't seen the commercials in a while, but I did run across a website (mormonchannel.org) with over a hundred of these clips. I watched a few and scanned through the rest. Boring.

Not one of them was truly a surprise because not one of them was anything other than average looking. Firefighter, nurse, athlete, surfer, amputee, pilot, musician, cop, social worker, etc.

The two things they all had in common were that they appeared giddily pleased with themselves, and they were Mormons.

The idea, I suppose, was to give the impression that Mormons are just regular folks like you. We're your coworkers, acquaintances, or even somebody you hit with your car. We're everywhere.

There's also the subtle message that you would fit right in with us. If an elementary school principal or an assembly line worker can be a Mormon, you could too.

Or not. Hey, I'm just saying that the commercials made us look safe enough to live next door.

I'm not impressed. I'm also a Mormon. If we're going to spend a huge amount of money on TV ads, why not target the people who could use a bit more church in their lives?

Hola, my name is Juan. I am an uncle, football enthusiast, and a guerilla fighter. *Tambien soy Mormon*."

If Juan's face was covered with a bandana and he was carrying an assault rifle, that would get your attention, right?

What about a guy with a shaved head and wearing an orange jump suit? "My name is Nick. I'm a father, a writer, and a death row inmate. I'm also a @%$& Mormon."

"My name is Misty. I'm a mother, a cookie baker, and a former adult film star. Ew. But I'm also a Mormon."

See? These are people who had the gospel transform their lives, or at least provided them with some balance in the lives they currently have. They're also people who are already "us" just like the pleasant ones in the commercials.

"My name is Grace. I'm a single mother, a grandmother, and I pull the guts out of turkeys at a processing plant. I'm also a Mormon."

"Hey there, I'm Roy. I'm an electrician, family man and Sasquatch hunter. I'm also—wait, what was that?!"

"Yo, I'm Mike. I'm a karate instructor and an undefeated cage fighter with over 200 knockouts. I'm Mormon. You got a problem with that?"

Mormons aren't just educated, hardworking people with regular lives. We can also be blackjack dealers, tattoo artists, Coca-Cola executives, sword swallowers, camel racers, emo/goth/skaters, wine makers, and even hemp growers.

"Hello, I'm Monica. I'm a psychic, a palm reader, and

an astrologer with 27 cats. I'm also a Mormon Sagittarius."

"Hey Ho. Kermit The Frog here…"

I'm kidding. Kermit's a Unitarian. But the LDS church needs a new and improved TV ad campaign, something that speaks to those of you (and us) who are really just like us. Or not.

"Hi, I'm Kirby. I'm happily married, a grandfather, an explosives enthusiast, and a rude newspaper columnist. Oh, and last time I checked, I'm also a Mormon."

SLT - January 11, 2014

33 A Dog's Life

My family lived in Spain until I was nine. When it was time to come home to America, I didn't want to leave. My parents promised me a dog. I wrote and asked my grandpa to find one.

"Dear Granpa. Please get me a dog. We will be home to soon on a airplane that dos not bomb. I am big now. Your grandson, Bobby Kirby. P.S. A dog thank you."

My grandfather Charlie was a profane and easily annoyed alcoholic. He didn't like people much, but he loved his oldest grandson. After he got my letter, Grandma said he drove around until he saw a good dog and stole it.

My first dog was a second-hand brown and white misdemeanor spaniel. She was waiting for me when we got to California. I named her Fontana. We took her with us to Boise, Idaho.

In a thank you letter to Charlie, I wrote that Boise was tolerable but Fontana was the world's best dog. I circled two of her muddy footprints on the page, and signed off, "Your beloved grandson Bobby Kirby. P.S. Please get me a boozooka."

I don't know if Fontana was the world's best dog. I certainly wasn't the world's best boy. But we were perfect for each other. We ran fields together, played in the snow, and caught pollywogs.

When I got my first "F," Fontana sat with me until the old man got home. She stayed with me the entire next two weekends in my room. That's loyalty.

We also stuck up for each other. She hated the bigger kid down the street who picked on me. After he kicked her, I waited an entire lunch hour to drop a garbage can on his head in a stairwell at school.

Fontana taught me about the miracle of life. She had puppies by Duncan's dog Petey—half a dozen wriggly little things that we had to give away. I always wondered if she missed them.

Dogs don't last as long as people. Some people don't last long either. Charlie and Fontana died within a year of each other. I can't remember who I cried harder for. I still have his letters and her collar.

I've had other dogs since Fontana: Baron, Lurch, Che, Chomper, Porky, Beau, Nena, Zoe and Scout. They are the slobbery, lop-eared milestones of my life. Each was beloved and every bit as neurotic as their owner.

On Monday, I had Scout put down. Old, arthritic and full of tumors, it was her time. We drove down to the vet's and I sat with her until her heart stopped and she was gone.

I tell myself that it was a favor; that she was getting crazy from the pain. But now I don't know what to do with my own. I got another dog's collar in my pocket and life hurts too much.

When I couldn't take it anymore, I put Scout's collar away. I wanted to forget as soon as possible. In the box was the thank you letter to Charlie. Fontana's muddy footprints are still visible after 45 years. I felt better.

A life measured by dogs hasn't been a waste of time.
SLT - November 28, 2007

34 **Wienermobile Driving**

On Friday, we took the famous Oscar Mayer Wienermobile up to the State Capitol and tried to park it in the legislative garage. Didn't work.

For one thing it wouldn't fit. Clearance to the capitol's parking garage is just over seven feet—four feet shorter than the Wienermobile is tall.

It didn't help that I had called Gov. Gary Herbert's office and formally requested an audience. The governor's assistant told us that the governor wasn't even in the state. We went anyway.

Two UHP troopers met us at the garage entrance and politely told us there was no Wienermobile parking at the State Capitol. We would have to leave.

TROOPER #1: "You can't park that thing in a fire lane."

ME: "This is an official temporary press vehicle and…"

TROOPER #2: "Taser him. Nobody will care."

We left the Capitol and went to LDS Church headquarters. The reception was a little better, although there was still a noticeable lack of Wienermobile parking. That didn't stop people from preventing us from leaving.

Tourists and LDS visitors who had come to see the Salt Lake Temple were instantly drawn to the sight. Cameras focused on the temple immediately swung around to capture the famous hotdog on wheels going past.

The rest of the tour around downtown went considerably better. People notice when you drive by in a giant hotdog. Cars honked. Kids waved. People walking dogs—including several dachshunds—stopped us to get pictures of their dogs with the Wienermobile.

Speaking of getting stopped, people aren't shy about standing in front of the Wienermobile in order to stop it so they can take pictures. They rightly figure that an enormous symbol of an American food staple won't run over them.

Near the Capitol, a woman blocked a driveway until we agreed to stop so that her entire family could pose with the rolling 27-foot hotdog. They left with free Wiener Whistles.

None of this behavior came as a surprise to professional Wienermobile drivers Ben Urkov (road name: Beefelicious Ben) and Jackie Calder (Pepper Jackie Cheese). The two "hotdoggers"—a reference to college graduates hired to drive the Wienermobile for a year—have seen everything.

Pepper Jackie and Beefelicious invited me along on the private downtown cruise. Inside, the Wienermobile is just as theme-driven as the exterior. The dashboard is shaped like a hotdog, the bun roof is removable, and the carpet resembles splattered condiments.

Urkov and Calder said that while the attention the Wienermobile draws is invariably positive, it took some getting used to at first. The two have driven the hot dog around the country since being hired in June.

They've never gotten a traffic ticket in the thousands of miles they've logged, but they have been stopped by the police who ask to have their picture taken with the Wienermobile.

Passing by a group of school kids leaving the Pioneer Memorial Museum, Ben hit the Wienermobile horn, a recording of the famous commercial jingle—"Oh, I wish I was an Oscar Mayer wiener." Many of the kids started singing along. It took me back.

The Wienermobile has graced American highways since it was invented in 1936. Hot Wheels issued two versions of it. The Wiener Whistle—which used to be included free in packages of hot dogs—came along the year before I was born.

I had a Wiener Whistle as a kid. Several of them in fact. All of them ended up on the American highway, where my father tossed them when he couldn't stand me playing them anymore in the back seat.

That's OK. Life is just one giant round. I came away from Friday's Downtown Wiener Tour with enough plastic Wiener Whistles for my grandkids. They can only play them in their grandmother's car though.

SLT - April 15, 2013

35 Collagen for Dessert

The human mind is a scary place. With hardly any effort, a single individual can think up something incredibly stupid and—here's the cool part—convince millions of other people that it's a good idea.

While this may sound like the beginning of another tiresome political or religious rant, it's not. I am in fact talking about boiling your grandma. And not just for the heck of it either. This is a serious column about dessert.

You didn't know that your grandma could be Jell-O, did you? It's true. In fact, practically any relative would work. You could also make gelatin out of a neighbor, a telemarketer, or even an extra hippopotamus you're not using.

Contrary to popular myth, the primary ingredient for Jell-O—collagen—does not come from cow hooves. Frankly, there isn't enough collagen in cow hooves to make a gummy bear, never mind fill a gelatin mold.

Dessert-grade gelatin, the kind strong enough to hold grapes and carrot bits in suspension, comes from an animal's hide and bones. Mostly cows and pigs, but also horses, moose, and left over actress lips.

I don't want to go into too much detail here about how gelatin is made. This is partly because many of you will be eating it soon— but mainly because some of you are loony enough to give it a try. I got into enough trouble over the catapult column.

Anyway, collagen is the primary ingredient in gelatin. It's what makes Jell-O gel. Without it, the stuff your crazy aunt throws into it would just sink to the bottom of the pan where it could be safely dodged.

I had an aunt who put—and I am absolutely not lying about this—tuna fish and capers in Jell-O. She called it Sunny Surf Salad. It looked and smelled like a koi pond but the old man made us eat it anyway.

Mercifully, I don't recall the taste. It was one of those dishes that takes a kid a year to eat because each bite had to be small enough to get it deep into your throat without accidentally tasting it.

If Sunny Surf Salad happened to touch a taste bud, it produced a gag reflex so powerful that your uvula stuck out of your mouth like a frog's tongue. A cousin knocked a picture off the wall.

People put all sorts of more acceptable things in Jell-O salad: fruit, vegetables, candy, tequila, etc. I'd eat one containing cigarette butts and wood screws before I'd touch another helping of Surf Salad.

Don't think you're dodging collagen by skipping Jell-O salads tomorrow. It's also in ice cream, yogurt, sour cream, marshmallows and, of course, the turkey.

SLT - November 26, 2008

36   **Life Round the Bend**

ROCK CREEK RANCH – In the growing light, a raft loaded with aging suburbanites slips past me in the current. Among the passengers, a woman snipes at her husband. Her voice is loud. It carries to the shore.

"I told you it would be like this. But you had to see it, didn't you?"

The Green River quickly carries the complainer around a bend and out of my life. I thank God for small mercies, and turn my attention to the towering cliffs.

Through the cottonwoods, the rising sun gradually illuminates the gorge. Every ten feet turns a million bygone years into gold.

I came to the river looking to escape life for a while and instead found it. The river carries real meaning that is easily missed if you're busy glaring at the back of someone else's head.

Nine new and old friends left the boat ramp at Sand Wash May 31 in a gusting wind. We were following in the wake of John Wesley Powell, who explored the canyon in 1869 and named it Desolation.

But ours is a different river. Powell navigated the Green at low water, every log jam and boulder a threat. Nearly 150 years later, the river is at flood stage and smothers many of the obstacles Powell faced.

There's still danger. At the moment we're setting off on what promises to be a carefree adventure, a woman is drowning at Wire Fence Rapid 60 miles ahead of us. The river, like life, is unforgiving.

Once you're in it, there's no going back on the river. Like life, the river is a journey of faith. You take what it serves up and do your best to handle your boat well. Much of the journey depends on your attitude. You'll find beauty or desolation.

We start slow, moving with a broad, deceptively sluggish current. The scenery is soon boring. Miles of tamarisk and mud drift past.

Like kids in the back seat, we pester our guides with hundreds of inane questions. What is that? Can we touch it? When are we going to get there? I have to go to the bathroom.

It happens soon enough, the first real challenge that alters our view of what's to come. We round a bend and pile into Rock House Rapid, a freezing, attention-getting slap of water. We bail it out and keep going.

There are dozens of these river altering moments ahead, times when clarity is forced on us. I can see them looking at a map, rapids with names like Fretwater, Cow Swim, Big Canyon, Wild Horse, Last Chance, Poverty and Surprise.

My life has been filled with such rapids, inexorable moments when the river narrows, cranks up, and it's sink or swim—Draft Notice, Marriage, First Born, Pink Slip, and Mortgage. I managed them with a little bit of preparation and a lot of faith.

If you're smart, you learn to anticipate those moments of alarm that punctuate the long stretches of calm in life. Listen closely and you can hear them coming.

On the river, you keep an ear cocked to the storm sound

of an approaching rapid. Boulders rolling underwater make a noise like a distant artillery duel. And there's the worst sound of all—the whistle of air leaving the raft.

What's that coming up? Is it just another Cough or is it Cancer? Disagreement or Divorce? If you aren't sure—and the current allows for it—you get out and go take a look.

We got out before Cow Swim and did that. Good thing, too. From the top of a boulder, the river boiled for a hundred yards. Rock-sharpened logs spun in the torrent. A raft hit a boulder and popped a tourist into the air.

There's no way around Cow Swim and nothing to take us through it but faith. We returned to the rafts, cinched our life vests just short of suffocation, and drove on. We make it soaked and shivering but oddly exhilarated. Some things are only fun when you can look back on them.

Faith is all in the seeing. It changes from person to person. Where some see only a gritty prison in the narrow canyon walls, others look and see sunlit houses of the holy.

Everywhere there are signs left by those who have gone before—petroglyphs and graffiti, flint chips and pull tabs, fossils and bottles. Eventually, my own passage will be added to the sediment of time.

In a moment of astonishing clarity, somewhere in the middle of a rapid, I realize that it's my birthday. I add my own paltry 58 years to the millions I see around me.

Life is a river. It doesn't stop moving just because you aren't paying attention. At night, I lay in my tent and listen to the water roll toward the Gulf of California 650 miles away. I'm reminded that I have a downriver destination of my own. And I'm already most of the way there.

Four days on the river and I learned there's beauty on the way to uncertainty. It's up to me to find it in whatever waits around the next bend.

SLT - June 14, 2011

37 **Scouting With the Master**

When I was a kid, I saw my Scoutmaster physically abuse a guy. It never got reported but it's an account that needs settling. I'm prepared to do that now.

Recent allegations in the news that the BSA covered up abuse by scout leaders in the past make this a timely column. People should get what they got coming to them. So here's what happened.

On a quiet summer evening in 1966, my scoutmaster punched a guy unconscious at a gas station in Beaver, Utah.

There were plenty of witnesses. Harold, Mikey, Leon, Duncan, Buddy, the Leavitt twins, and I all saw it happen. Calvin didn't because he was still in the restroom.

We stopped in Beaver because it was 200 miles from home to Puffer Lake. After three hours padlocked in Ray's camper, eight boys desperately needed a bathroom.

We were climbing back into the camper when a pickup pulled in behind us. A woman jumped out crying. A cursing guy followed her out and grabbed her arm.

Things probably would have been OK except the man hit the gal. Ray yelled at him but the guy drew back his fist again.

There was a loud crack and the guy went down like every fuse in his head had been tripped. He didn't even twitch.

Ray suggested the woman call the cops. Instead she

mumbled her thanks, got back in the pickup and left. So did we.

Ray went into the bathroom and came out lugging Calvin. He threw him into the camper with the rest of us, locked the door, and we were on the highway again.

CALVIN: "What'd I miss?"

HAROLD: "Ray killed somebody."

Sitting around a campfire later that evening, a chagrinned Ray tried explaining the concept of chivalry to a collection of grubby trolls.

RAY: "You guys understand what I'm saying?"

DUNCAN: "Yeah. If we're mean to girls, you'll kill us, too."

Ray committed other abuses during his reign as our Scoutmaster. He once hiked us three miles without Kool-Aid to a ranger station to apologize after we chopped a tree down across a highway.

And he was into bondage. At various times Ray chained one or more of us to a fence, the bumper of his truck, a tree stump, picnic table, and a forest service sign. I don't know about other fathers, but mine told him that he could.

There was a certain amount of hypocrisy in Ray's abusive behavior. For example, he sometimes cussed. But he also burned our girlie magazines, fireworks, cigarettes, and a patrol flag we made out of an enormous brassiere we stole from another camp.

Oh, and he was maliciously hygienic. If he caught us peeing anywhere other than a latrine, he would summarily sling us into the lake or a creek.

Finally there was real physical abuse, known among us as "Ray-Aid." Fishhooks, animal bites, food poisoning, sprains, cuts—there wasn't any injury so severe that Ray couldn't fix it with a long finger, a bottle of Bactine, and a pair of pliers.

I can't vouch for what went on in other BSA troops. I only know that the treatment we received had a lasting effect on us: two cops, bank vice-president, general contractor, lawyer, musician, and a college professor.

Hell, who knows what we could have become if we hadn't suffered this abuse at the hands of a Boy Scout leader?

SLT - September 19, 2012

38   His Holiness The Kirb

I entered the ministry last week. After much study and thought, I became an ordained Christian pastor. Yeah, it freaked my mom out, too. I haven't told my bishop yet.

Exactly what led me to accept this path is a bit complicated. We'll get into that in a minute. First, how it was done.

Keep in mind that the ministry isn't for everyone. Only those with 99 bucks and access to the Internet. I went online to The Holy Christian Church website, paid them, and they sent me a certificate of recognition in the mail. Check it out.

There was a test. Fortunately, it was only three questions long. And they were more like statements. Did I believe in God, Jesus Christ, and had I repented for my sins?

Next to each of the questions/statements were boxes that had to be checked. A checked box indicated a "yes" answer. An unchecked box was a "no." Since there wasn't a box for, "It's OK with me," I checked all three.

At the end of the test (on which I got 100), was the final caution: "If you have not yet prayed for forgiveness of your sins, please take a moment to do so now before giving us your credit card number."

NOTE: It's also possible to become a rabbi or an imam this way. I picked Christian because it's the one with which I'm most familiar. And if I'm going to hell for it, I want it to be

Christian hell. I'm not learning some whole other language of damnation.

A week later, I got my certificate in the mail. I hung it on the wall and set about the business of being a Christian pastor.

What? Yes, even though I'm really a Mormon.

My qualifications? Well, I don't know. I suppose people expect a minister to have some sort of formal training, a degree from a divinity school or the like.

If I scraped all of my training together, I would say three years of LDS seminary (two of them early morning), couple of years as a missionary, the police academy, and 37 years of marriage gives me a ministerial doctorate in getting the [stuff] kicked out of me by life.

I don't feel at a disadvantage. Lots of other people got into this business with less and did OK. Plenty of others got into it with more—and really screwed it up.

I'll need a title. For now, you may refer to me as Pastor Kirb. His Holiness Kirby the Second also works. So does the Right Reverend Rob, Bad Shepherd, Deacon of Doom, and Bishop Mayhem. Hey, there's no reason this can't be fun.

Anyway, I'm a man of the cloth now. Whatever that really means. To me (and you) it means I can now organize a congregation, accept tithes, counsel lost sheep, hear confessions, and sell indulgences.

NOTE: I'm not absolutely sure about that last one. I'll have to do some checking. If it works out, I'll post a fee schedule here.

I know what you're thinking—"That Kirby isn't a real Christian pastor."

The hell I'm not. In addition to the certificate (in a frame with real glass), I have a white shirt I can wear backwards, AND I can legally marry people.

That's right.

I called Salt Lake County Clerk Sherrie Swenson to see if my ordination was good. She said that I'm fully OK to join people in holy matrimony.

ME: "Woohoo!"

SHERRIE: "Your credentials are good. I'm not sure you are."

I'll perform my first wedding in September, when I ask Brook if she takes Nate to be her awfully wedded husband.

Clearly, I'll need to practice before then.

SLT - June 23, 2012

39　Talking Turkey Trash

As many of you know, Saturday morning was the beginning of a deeply spiritual weekend for many Utahns. They gathered together to worship and learn how to talk turkey.

While the rest of the state went to LDS General Confurnz, hundreds of turkey hunters congregated at the Deseret Peak Complex in Tooele for the second annual National Wild Turkey Federation banquet.

Before you start thinking, "Hey, I thought all our turkeys were in Washington, D.C.," understand that Utah is home to thousands of wild turkeys. You never see them because wild turkeys are in fact highly efficient CIA operatives.

Do not confuse wild turkeys with grocery store turkeys. Wild turkeys are much smarter than mass produced turkeys, which escape being classified as a species of squash only by the fact that they have feet.

Saturday morning found me in a turkey-calling seminar conducted by Lynn Worwood, of Nephi, a member of the nationally recognized Quaker Boy calling team.

Turkey calling turned out to be way different than hog calling, which pretty much amounts to standing on a back porch and bellowing something the hog has been conditioned to associate with food. In the nation's capitol, this is referred to as a "tax dollar holler."

To call a wild turkey, you have to sound exactly like a turkey. This is way harder than it appears because wild turkeys are on the same paranoia level as Michael Jackson.

The idea behind turkey calling is to lure the turkey close enough to shoot him for dinner. You want the turkey as close as possible when this happens because you need to shoot it in the head, and a turkey's head is about the size of a small pointy walnut.

You never shoot a turkey in the body. If you have to ask why, buy a frozen turkey dinner, sprinkle liberally with gravel, cook, and eat. Notice how it has the same effect as having your dental work done with a roller skate key.

Unless he happens to be more of a genetic oddity than other turkey hunters, it's impossible to duplicate turkey calls with the human larynx. Worwood demonstrated a number of turkey calling devices, including a turkey cell phone.

Using a small wooden contraption known as a "box call," Worwood produced a sound that perfectly mimicked Aunt Beulah hopelessly stuck in the bathtub. According to him, this was wild turkey for, "Hey, sailor."

Even though wild turkeys have a brain about the size of a pea, they are not easily fooled by artificial calls. That's because 94 percent of a turkey's brain is completely devoted to turkey caller ID.

So, if you make the wrong turkey noise, it shows up on the turkey's caller ID as, "overweight human with large gun." When that happens, Tom does not stop running until Pocatello.

Speaking of which, wild turkeys can run up to 30 mph. Since only hunters pursued by bears are capable of reaching this speed, and there is never a bear on a turkey hunt when you need one, do not waste your time.

Turkey talk amounts to about 30 different sounds, most

of them focused on the subject of getting lucky. A scratchy hiccup, two squeaks, and something that sounds like a drunk rat yodeling on helium, means:

"Financially secure single Tom seeks single finely feathered hen into nesting, gobbling and enthusiastic egg making. Also some light bondage."

Learning how to speak turkey is not something you can learn overnight, or even at the LDS Missionary Training Center in Provo. It's actually more of an art form.

Like all art forms, including newspaper column writing, turkey calling requires two things: a lunatic and a lot of time.

SLT - April 3, 2001

40   **Waiting on Eternity**

If you are not thinking about killing yourself, you might want to read something else today. If you are, please read this first. It will only take a few minutes.

In the extremity of whatever's bothering you enough to make death attractive, there is something you may not have considered. Give it a think while you can still do something about it.

I got to know a lot of dead people as a cop. Old age, murder, crashes, falls; human beings check out in a variety of ways. I've seen most of them up close enough to get some of it on me.

Suicides bothered me the most. They still do. It's been years since I eased open the door of a darkened room and saw someone with a shotgun between their legs and their head all over the ceiling. But some things you see for the rest of your life.

That part of my police memory is a photo album of the hopelessly sad with shattered skulls, elongated necks, and bile-soaked faces. Sometimes I can still smell them.

It was my job back then to visit the nightmares people made of themselves in basements, garages, and bedrooms. I even got used to it in a twisted way. They were strangers. Mostly.

If you kill yourself, odds are that it won't be a stranger

who finds you. It will be someone concerned enough to look for you in the first place: your mother, your child, your spouse, or some other unfortunate who shouldn't have seen you like that but did.

People kill themselves for a variety of reasons. The one I'm most familiar with is selfishness. I read enough suicide notes to know that the authors were generally no crazier than I and perhaps no more depressed.

Just because someone does something horrible doesn't mean that they couldn't help it. It means that they arrived at the point where what they wanted was more important to them than what other people deserved, including those who love them.

Sometimes it's deliberate. I sat with a corpse once and read his journal while we waited for the medical examiner. The last entry was: "I hope the insurance makes you happy."

The guy had been lucid enough to drive to his former living room and put the muzzle of a deer rifle into his mouth believing that the next person who found him would be his estranged wife. He was wrong. It was his ten-year-old daughter. And she didn't give a damn about the insurance.

Just because you'll be more careful won't make it easier for a loved one to take. Trust me, there is no clean way to kill yourself. Pills? Exhaust? Please. No one covered in her own vomit looks peaceful.

I didn't think human beings could scream as long and as loud as the woman who found her teenage son hanging in his bedroom, his face the color of an eggplant. That will always be her last memory of him.

A friend left me with a similar sight. When he didn't show up for work, I went to his house and found him. The burden of life was too much for Ron, so he added to mine.

When I recall his face now, I'm invariably reminded that he didn't have one.

It's a terrible thing to do to strangers, too. Later, when I interviewed the engineer of a train after a woman deliberately stepped in front of it, I knew from the look in his eyes that he would never stop leaning on the brakes.

Suicide does not make the problem better, only bigger. It spreads your pain to everyone who ever cared about you and even to people who haven't met you yet. If that isn't what you want, then suicide isn't either.

If you're still thinking about it, please give yourself a little more time to reconsider. There's no rush. It's not like eternity will leave without you.

SLT - May 13, 2006

NOTE: Not my usual irreverent self in this one. It won an award from the Society of Professional Journalists.

41 No Place to Park City

Saturday night was the Sundance Film Festival showing of a remake of the Ashton Kutcher film, "Dude, Where's My Car?" Easily four stars.

Produced and directed by the Park City Police department, it has drama, heartache, eye-popping rage, and riveting suspense.

The show began just after dark, when half the population of earth showed up at Park City Mountain Resort for the second round of the snowboard halfpipe finals. They all needed someplace to park.

But there aren't any places to park during the film festival, at least none that are convenient. Parking wherever is the central conflict in "Dude, Where's My Car 2."

As the plot developed, residents began calling the police to report their driveways blocked or occupied by vehicles that didn't belong to them. City bus drivers couldn't maneuver through the choked streets.

The main feeder routes became one-way (barely) lanes when drivers simply abandoned their vehicles at any vacant spot close to the resort.

My seat for this epic drama was in a Park City police patrol vehicle. When dispatched to fix the problem, it took us the better part of half an hour to get to the scene less than five blocks away.

When we arrived, the intersection looked like a used car lot for the mentally deranged. Vehicles were parked on private property, under "No Parking" signs, in lanes of travel, on corners, and up on piles of snow.

The solution was immediately apparent: a tow truck. A bunch of them. Half a dozen showed up and fought their way through the congestion.

TOW DRIVER: "How many?"

OFFICER: "That one, those three over there, the two in this line, that other one, and everything on that side of the road. Don't forget that Beamer."

The tow truck drivers got to work. I was impressed. It looked impossible considering how tightly wedged some of the vehicles were.

Towing cars is three parts physics, two parts proper equipment, and three parts art form. A truly talented tow operator can pull a car with its doors open from the bottom of a well without scratching it.

The offending vehicles ranged from old Motor City beaters to high-end foreign rockets. Pedigrees didn't matter. They all came sideways out of their spots, then winched onto a wrecker, and were hauled away. That's when the show got really interesting.

Apparently word got out that the cops were stealing cars. People started to hurry back. In some cases they arrived in the nick of time. But more than a few didn't.

I was watching the tow drivers when a young man hurried out of the darkness and said, "Dude, where's my car?"

OFFICER: "It left with a tow truck."

KID: "Will they bring it back?"

This was not the dumbest thing said in the next hour. In descending order of dumbest, they were:

"I didn't see any parking signs," a guy insisted. He was referred to the large red and white "No Parking Any Time" sign on the pole above where his car used to be.

"Taking someone's car without their permission is rude," a woman cried. Maybe, but parking in the roadway is illegal.

"Everyone else was parking here, too," an older man snarled. And their cars got towed, too.

The illegally parked cars were towed away. Order was restored. Traffic got back to its normal Sundance pace: crawling. It was beautiful.

There's still time to land a supporting role at the Film Festival. Drive to Park City and leave your ride...oh, just anywhere. They'll find you.

SLT - January 21, 2014

42   Suburban Water Torture

May is here. According to weather forecasters, now is a good time to turn on your automatic lawn sprinklers to see if your anti-depressant medication really works.

First, turn on the main water valve. This will give you a general idea how the system faired during the winter. Based on this you can then decide whether any repairs need to be made or if it's time to let the bank foreclose.

The formula is simple: Times each waterspout shooting from the ground, by a month and 450 bucks. Add ten thousand dollars for each spout having a diameter equal to that of a fire hose.

Lots of things happen to a sprinkling system during the winter. The pipes can freeze and break. The sprinkler heads might get knocked off by a snow thrower, or gnawed loose by a bored dog soon to have all the hair beat off of it.

Worse, you could have spent the winter months simply imagining that you had an automatic sprinkling system.

Do not turn on the water to your sprinkling system then immediately rush over to peer into a sprinkler head. The system—assuming that it still works—will expel lots of air and foreign matter. Nothing takes the fun out of spring like getting hit in the face with high-speed mole.

Next, check the valve boxes. Pull off the cover, bat away the cobwebs, thrust your head into the hole and immediately become an atheist. Invariably a valve has broken and must be fixed.

Repairing a broken valve requires digging up part of your home's foundation and cutting the damaged part out. No matter how frustrated you may become here, never resort to dynamite, prayer, or, worse, a neighbor's advice.

Remove the broken valve. You are now ready to make the first of innumerable trips for parts. The trick here is to never confuse the hardware store with a bar.

Fortunately, the automatic sprinkler genome has already been mapped and plotted by genetic engineers. All you need to know is which parts fit where, something no more complicated than a liver transplant.

The good news is that repairing a sprinkling system is easy for anyone with advanced degrees in hydrodynamics, civil engineering and PVCology.

PVC is, of course, the kind of pipe used in sprinkling systems. Typically it is white, sturdy and relatively inexpensive. You can find it at any hardware store or by trolling for it in your yard with a power tiller.

Sadly, even if you need to splice a five-inch piece, PVC pipe is only sold in lengths longer than an election year. It will test all your ingenuity to get them home in a Nissan Sentra.

It's best if you take the damaged part to the store. That way you can show it to a high school age clerk who will thoughtfully examine it at length and conclude, "Whoa."

Return home with the new part(s). Make certain that they don't fit. Pitch a teeth-splintering fit. Head back to the store. Curse and repeat until dark.

Ironically, if everything goes well, your sprinkling system should be back on line at exactly the moment when local governments ban their use because of the drought.

SLT - May 6, 2004

43   **Right Person, Wrong Place**

On an April morning in 1973, my father pulled the family Plymouth up to a curb in downtown Salt Lake City and ordered me out.

HIM: "Good luck. Don't come home until 1975."

ME: "OK, let me get my suitcase--."

The old man shot the car away from the curb like I might change my mind. Had I known what was coming, I probably would have.

At that moment I was just one of nearly a thousand white shirts being funneled into the old North Temple mission home, 30 seconds into what 40 years later I still consider the worst two months of my entire life.

It didn't take long for me to realize that I was out of my element. Less than 24 hours after walking through the front door, I penned this spiritual lament in my new missionary journal:

"Monday, April 23 – Everyone talks about their mission calls and how happy they are to be here. I like my call OK, but I [deleted] hate this [deleted] place."

Some of what I was feeling was my fault. In the days before the missionary bar was raised, it was possible to go from being a petty criminal to a servant of the Lord in a matter of weeks. I know because I did it.

Lack of preparation aside, a large part of how I was

feeling about the mission home wasn't my fault. It was place versus personality, and not all environments are suited for all people no matter how you try to correlate the two.

I wasn't opposed to being correlated per se. By the time I walked into the mission home I'd already been in the Army and jail. I'd been correlated plenty.

But neither of those had prepared me for the emotional claustrophobia of religious group think. It's one thing to order people to stand in a line and another to try and make them feel unworthy for not liking it.

One of the first things said to me as I entered the mission home was, "Elder, the Lord would be very disappointed in your haircut."

Since even then I didn't believe it was possible to disappoint an omnipotent being, I figured this was just a self-important way of telling me my hair was too long. Fine, I'll get another haircut. But why drag God into it?

Pointing this out was not appreciated. Neither was any other expressed lack of enthusiasm for the wonders of gang spirituality.

Whether its beads, khakis, or white shirts, few people are more brainlessly enthusiastic than kids with a mandate and a uniform. You can get them to do—and feel—just about anything, including unworthiness.

What followed was two months of eating, sleeping, studying, and emoting in unison in order to be validated. It wasn't me.

It wasn't a few other guys either. I watched them become sullen, then livid, and once or twice, self-injurious for their failure to adapt in a highly cloistered—and artificial—environment.

They weren't the wrong people. Just in the wrong

place. The great fear was that losing yourself in the Lord's work meant becoming something you weren't.

I survived the missionary training center and was sent to South America. On the day I left, I wrote:

"Toosday, June 26 – We took our luggage down to the van for the airport. I did 66 days of this crap. That's one 6 short of the mark of the beast. It's a sign I think. Good riddance."

The rest of my mission went better. There was still a lot of work to do. One of the toughest jobs there is in life is be yourself when you're stuck in the middle of everyone else.

SLT - July 20, 2013

44 Coping with the Faithful

I got recognized on TRAX last week. It was early morning and I was sitting across from an older couple dressed for Temple Square or the LDS church office building.

You know what I mean—white shirt, prim dress, necktie, conservative haircut, etc. Yeah, fellow Mormons.

My fellow Mormons didn't quite have me figured out yet. I could tell they were working on it though. They whispered and stared whenever they thought I wasn't looking.

When I moved aside to let someone through the aisle, the words *"The Salt Lake Tribune"* became visible on my bag. That did it. The woman's lips instantly thinned in disapproval.

HER: "You're the one who writes those rude articles about the church."

ME: "Pat Bagley, ma'am. Pleased to meet you."

Merle and LaDawn (names I invented, but are probably real close) weren't exactly pleased to meet me. During the next couple of minutes they struggled to remain Christ-like while still giving me a piece of their collective mind.

The woman said she knew all about me. Her daughter, who was in danger of losing her testimony, routinely sent them links to my Faith column in the hope of offending them.

It worked. They *were* offended. They were offended that someone who would write the things I did would actually go to church and claim to be Mormon. The woman ran through a quick list of objections to past columns.

Using the term "Nazi Mormon" was an insult to faithful members of the church. It wasn't a sin for Mormons to lick our lips on Fast Sunday. There was no such thing as "13 Particles of Faith" in any church book she had ever read.

Knocking on doors with a dog dressed like a missionary was wrong. General Authorities spoke the way they did in Conference because they were led by the Spirit, not because they had been to a Holy Ghost finishing school.

Finally, the woman had been a Primary President and would have me know that the noise generated by Mormon children in Sacrament meeting didn't sound anything at all like Tasering monkeys in a parking garage.

There was a lot more. When she finally paused for breath, her husband added his two cents, "Hey, you aren't Pat Bagley."

I conceded that some of what they said might be true. Heavenly Father's mother-in-law probably wasn't Satan, and it was possible that the Savior really would be wearing a Mr. Mac suit and a necktie in the Second Coming.

"Then you shouldn't try and make people think otherwise," the woman said, triumphantly. "You're hurting the church. You and our daughter should ask yourselves why you do it."

I knew the answer to that already. It was, frankly, an easy one. Her daughter would probably even agree with it.

"It's how Mormons like us cope going to church with Mormons like you."

That was the end of the Christ-like part of conversation. The couple got off in a huff at the next stop. We weren't even at Temple Square yet.

I try to avoid these kinds of gospel discussions. Not

only do they frequently end up sounding like bishop interviews, but someone always gets their feelings hurt. And it's never me.

SLT - September 21, 2013

45 **Ringing For Help**

I rang a bell for the Salvation Army Wednesday night. Two hours in the freezing cold wasn't so bad, but I'll hear that bell in my sleep for months.

The Salvation Army's annual Red Kettle drive raises money to feed the homeless, care for children, help seniors and provide relief in disasters. It's also a good opportunity for overfed and overpaid people like me to lend a hand.

Any fool can wear a red apron and bother people with a bell. The idea is to get the public to notice you without making them mad. It's an art.

The bell ringer I replaced at the kettle in front of Smith's, 10350 S. 1300 East, was young and—well, that was enough. He wore a set of headphones that shut out the world. His bell handling was grim to the point of attempted robbery.

I adopted a more casual approach, ringing the bell just enough to get shoppers' attention. And since I didn't have any headphones (ear muffs, or ears after two hours), I could hear what they said.

"Thanks for ringing the bell, man."

"Please stop doing that. This is an important call."

"Dad, it's that newspaper guy Mom hates!"

I could also haggle. Some guy offered 10 bucks if I would stop long enough for him to get to his car in peace and quiet. We settled on $20 and a muffin.

One woman said thanks weren't necessary because, "The Salvation Army saved my brother's life." Another wept silently while searching her purse for every single coin she could find.

An elderly man in a thin jacket hobbled all the way back out to his car and returned with eight pounds of spare change. When I asked if he was cold, he said, "Not since Korea."

A drunk tried to put a cigarette butt in the kettle. Friends steered him to a garbage can instead. It took 40+ tries for him to fit a five dollar bill into the slot while simultaneously apologizing.

When traffic was slow, I sold bell ringing opportunities to little kids for a dollar a minute. One really enthusiastic kid shook the clapper out of the bell and we had to fix it. I didn't mind. After an hour of ringing, the temporary silence was a narcotic.

Not everyone gave. The opportunity caught some off guard. Others probably had their own favorite charities. But plenty of people heard the ringing and paused to search themselves for whatever they could find. They wouldn't have if it hadn't been for my noise.

I still have this nagging ring in my ear. If I'm lucky it'll stay there long enough to do me and someone else some good.

SLT - November 24, 2007

46 Excommunication for the Dead

With the revelation that President Obama's mama may now be a Mormon, the LDS practice of baptism for the dead is once again in the news.

Ann Dunham, who died in 1995, was subsequently baptized by proxy in an LDS temple. Mormons believe that Mrs. Dunham would need this ordinance when she got to the other side.

President Obama hasn't commented on the matter. However, according to my double secret source inside the White House, he might have said, "If I didn't care what Mormons thought when I was running for president, why would I care now?'

Mormons tend to see baptism for the dead as a personal favor rather than spiritual conscription. It's not as if you have to accept it. This life or the next, you're perfectly within your right to shout obscenities at us and slam the door.

But baptism for the dead makes a whole lot more sense than the afterlife plan some faiths have – which is that you go straight to hell if you didn't see it their way before you died.

At least with Mormons there's a second chance. And if we end up being right, you just might be grateful for that baptism.

What's that? You'd sooner go to hell than become Mormon? OK, but Hell isn't very pleasant. I got a hundred bucks that says an eternity of sponge bathing Hitler will change your mind.

This assumes, of course, that Mormons are in charge on the other side. Frankly, even though I'm Mormon, I don't think we will be. I believe God will be in charge—and that we're all of us (you included) in for a big fat surprise.

On the other hand, it's easy to see how some people don't like the idea of Mormons giving their dearly departed an ecclesiastical makeover. In the wake of angry protests, the church has agreed to stop doing it.

But what about those baptisms for the dead we've already performed? After all, you can't simply unbaptize someone, right?

Actually, that's not exactly true. If you're upset that Grandpa may have become Mormon on the other side, I can help. It's called Excommunication for the Dead.

I thought it up several years ago but got into trademark trouble with the church. They're not interested in it anymore, so I'm back in business. Here's how it works.

For an appropriate consideration, I can get your ancestor's baptism for the dead thrown out. It won't be free though. There's serious effort involved.

For $250 bucks, I'm willing to commit some horrible proxy sin on behalf of your ancestor that will get him (or her) excommunicated from the LDS church. For example, I specialize in lusting in my heart.

It says right in the Bible that gazing upon a woman with lust in your heart is the same thing as committing the actual act. This is a huge ecclesiastical loophole, people.

NOTE: My wife and Jenifer Aniston don't think lusting in my heart is the same thing as the actual deed, but we're talking about what the Lord thinks.

Send me Grandpa's name, a certified check, and the woman you want the proxy sin committed with, and I'll get right to work. I'm a professional, so it won't take longer than the average church meeting.

If it's Grandma, I can still help. I commit murder in my heart every time I drive to work. It's easy. By the time I get to the Tribune, she'll be a mass murderer and no longer a candidate for becoming Mormon.

For your money, you'll receive an attractive certificate of proxy excommunication worthy of framing. Simply present the certificate to whoever is in charge on the other side.

Unless it's the Mormons. If that's the case, then we're both in a lot of trouble.

SLT - May 9, 2009

47 Home Teaching Lessons

I try to get my home teaching done every month. Doesn't always work out that way. Lots of excuses for not doing it. My favorite is that I just don't feel like going.

For non-Mormons, home teaching is an LDS member visiting program wherein a couple of guys from the ward drop in once a month to see how you're doing.

Recipients of these visits regard them in a variety of ways: a welcome spiritual moment, an annoying interruption, actual spying for the bishop, etc.

The tenor of the visit depends largely on the personality of the home teachers. It can be a solemn mini-lesson on some church topic, or just a cookie munching bull session that basically verifies the family is alive.

Anyway, home teaching is a semi-big deal for Mormons. You hope the families you're assigned to visit are cool, and you hope your own home teachers aren't a couple of tedious scripture squirrels.

A couple of weeks ago I was assigned a new family to home teach. Actually it was just one guy. I'll call him Junior because that's his name.

Junior is a recognizable character in our neighborhood. He lives four doors down the street from me. We first met when his Rottweiler wandered into my kitchen for a drink.

Although technically LDS, Junior has only come to

church once. He's much more active in drugs, crime, alcohol, domestic violence, and the occasional police raid. He's been to jail at least three times that I know about.

His yard is equally colorful, sort of Appalachian holler retro. At any given moment, a half dozen disabled cars occupy the driveway. Automotive parts, tools, building supplies, old appliances fill up the rest of the space.

Here's the thing. Junior is a nice guy. I like him. He's helpful, friendly and interesting. He knows I'm an ex-cop and I know he's an occasional felon. Doesn't seem to get in our way though.

I saw him out in his yard last week. I pulled over to let him know that my HT partner and I'd be coming by to visit once a month. Thoroughly pierced, inked and baked, he was still interesting to talk to. We chatted about life in general until he abruptly stopped and apologized.

Him: "S*&#, man. Sorry for f%$&@ swearing."

Me: "Junior, I'm your f%$&@ home teacher, not the language police."

We fist bumped and agreed to get together later in the week. It didn't work out. While I was looking forward to visiting Junior, so were the cops.

Seems my new home teaching assignment borrowed someone else's vehicle and their debit card. UPD raided his house with a warrant and hauled a bunch of stuff away, including Junior. Then the health department sealed the home as uninhabitable.

I'll probably have to go visit Junior in jail now. Or I could just count the drive-by as a visit. Technically I did stop by to see him.

Doesn't matter. I have my own new home teacher worries now. A few days ago, new ward members "Bill" and his son dropped by some cookies and introduced themselves as our new home spies...I mean, teachers.

Bill knows I work for *The Salt Lake Tribune,* and that I'm not entirely rational. Meanwhile, he works full-time in a highly responsible position at LDS Church headquarters.

Hmm, this could get really complicated.

SLT - August 2, 2014

48 Homecoming at Skyline

Robert Kirby

This is what an idiot looked like in the spring of 1971. It's my senior yearbook picture. I thought you ought to know since that's where I'm taking you.

On Friday, I did something I swore 33 years ago to never do again. I went back to Skyline High School. As usual, I was being sent to the principal's office.

Walking into Skyline was a strange plunge down a rabbit hole. The halls, lockers, doors and even the smell were the same, but I had suddenly aged and swelled.

For a moment it seemed that my best friend Bruce Hepworth, dead from cancer these many years, was right there with me looking for trouble again. We weren't really bad kids, or at least Hep wasn't. Mostly we were just bored by school.

But bad enough that I still remembered my way to the principal's office. I got the sweats walking into it. I kept expecting the ghosts of Mr. Pizza and Mr. Middleton to shake their heads and ask, "What now?"

There were other more tangible ghosts in the office, including Ted Wilson a Skyline social studies teacher during my incarceration. Ted later went on to fame as mayor of Salt Lake, a mountain climber, political consultant, ski bum, and is currently advising Mayor Rocky Anderson.

Ted was enormously popular among students for being not only a good teacher but a "groovy" guy as well. The groovy part served me well.

Shortly before graduation, I was hauled before the slacker committee with a grade point average that suggested my school years would have been better served in Special Ed.

Mr. Wilson was on the committee. After a brief interview, Mr. Wilson apparently decided to let life work me over rather than keep me in school. He put my file on the "graduating" pile and I was free.

Then there was Coach Ken Schmidt, a former college all-star and NFL jock. He drove Skyline's football team to countless victories before spending years as the defensive coordinator for the BYU Cougars.

The coach doesn't remember me. I remember him. Once, when I was blocking an aisle in the locker room, he lifted me up and out of his way by the back of my gym shorts.

He also caught a group of us smoking behind the gym one wintry day. Instead of busting us, Coach shouted that he would appreciate the hell out of it if we worked on killing ourselves somewhere other than his football field.

Since Coach Schmidt was the Skyline faculty member voted least likely to take any crap whatsoever from a bunch of skinny creeps, we galloped in the direction of the parking lot.

On Friday, I shook hands with Ted and Ken and Skyline Principal Kathy Clark, who led us down to the auditorium for the Homecoming assembly. The exact same seats where Hep and I once sat bored out of our skulls are still there.

In an hour-long assembly, the tireless educator, the

winning coach, and the newspaper hack were inducted into Skyline High School's Hall of Fame.

One of us could hear Hep laughing all the way from the back of the auditorium.

SLT - October 18, 2004

49   Keeping Your Own Faith

Following last week's column on the miserable job I'm doing obeying the Ten Commandments, a reader suggested that it was high time that I renounce my membership in the LDS church.

"You aren't doing a good job obeying the Articals [sic] of Faith either. Why don't you leave the church for once and all because you aren't being a true member if you don't want to have faith like the rest of us."

It's true. I *don't* want to "have faith like the rest of" you. I couldn't even if I did. I'm not wired that way. Fortunately, I don't have to be for faith to work.

I sent the woman a copy of Elder Jeffrey R. Holland's recent conference talk ("Lord, I Believe"), in which Elder Holland said, "I am not asking you to pretend to faith you do not have. I <u>am</u> asking you to be true to the faith you do have."

If that isn't recognition that people aren't the same when it comes to faith, I don't know what is. What I do know is that it's OK for me to have doubts so long as I focus on what works for me.

To solidify this point, I also sent the woman a copy of my "13 Particles of Faith," a personal manifesto against cloned worship. The 11th Particle of Faith reads:

"I claim the privilege of worshiping Almighty God according to it being none of your &%#@ business, and allow all men the same privilege except megachurch pastors, self help gurus, and some cannibals."

The woman immediately fired back with "unfaithful" and "unspiritual." I'll go out on a limb here and assume that she was referring to me rather than Elder Holland. The Lord's anointed or the spiritually disjointed, apparently neither piece worked for her. But since it leaves me in good company (for once), I'm good.

When it comes to matters of faith about anything, it's important to play to your strengths. I didn't always know this.

It took a long time to figure out that faith is a deeply personal matter and I could drive myself nuts trying to fit someone else's circus under my tent. So I stopped.

Faith isn't what I stopped. I stopped stressing about the things I didn't have much faith in and focused instead on what did it for me. It was amazing how fast it took for the rest to matter less.

Ironically, I don't just get this zero tolerance, everybody-the-same, all-or-nothing faith logic from fellow church goers.

I also get it from ex-Mormons, non-Mormons, and anti-Mormons, people every bit as insistent on correlating my faith. If I don't agree with everything at church why would I believe anything? I should leave with them.

"I don't understand how a liberal thinking guy like you can actually be a Mormon."

That's easy. My pathologically unsynchronizeable brain believes that the eleventh Particle of Faith works on them just as well.

Maybe it's just me but I don't believe everything about anything or anyone. I don't even believe my wife when she says something like, "Well, we don't have the money for that."

It's a lie. We probably do have the money. I just don't know where it is. And since she isn't going to tell me, it works out to me taking it on faith.

Here's the thing. I don't plan on leaving her over this major issue. I focus on what she says that I can believe, and the amazing things she brings to my life when she isn't making me crazy. Apparently there's enough of that because we aren't penniless and divorced.

I'm still married, still going to church, still working, and still a citizen. I even still have a few friends. Wow. All of that from focusing on the parts I do have faith in.

SLT - April 20, 2013

50   **My Particles of Faith**

1. I believe in God, Jesus Christ, the Holy Ghost, and in mankind's inability to tell the difference between them and a giant ball of fire or an extremely intolerant political party.
2. I believe that men will be punished for their own transgressions, including stuff we did completely by accident or because of testosterone. Women will probably just get probation.
3. I believe that through the atonement of Christ, everyone will one day be able to tell annoying church leaders where to get off.
4. I believe that the first principles and ordinances of the church are boring speakers, meetings that last forever, music that sounds like whale sonograms, food storage gone bad, and idiotic bickering over caffeine and movie ratings.
5. I believe that a man must be called by God, by prophecy, and by the laying on of hands, by those who are in authority, and that Facebook posts and texting do not apply. Meanwhile, women answer only to a biological clock.
6. I believe in the same organization that existed in the Primitive Church, viz.: deacons, teachers, centurions,

lepers, thieves, virgins, lunatics, mustard seeds, and demonically possessed swine.

7. I believe in the gift of tongues and would die a happy man if, just once, some smartass would have the guts to try it when I was around.

8. I believe the Bible and the Book of Mormon to be the word of God as far as I personally can translate them correctly, which I try not to do because it scares me.

9. I believe all that God has revealed, all that He does now reveal, and I believe he will yet reveal many great and important things pertaining to the colossal foolishness of the entire human race.

10. I believe in the literal gathering of Israel and in the restoration of the Ten Tribes, most of whom will work for Microsoft; that the New Jerusalem will be built on this (the United States) continent by undocumented migrant labor, and that Christ will eventually rain personality on a generally colorless church.

11. I claim the privilege of worshiping Almighty God according to it being none of your &%#@ business, and allow all men the same privilege, except for mega-church pastors, self-help gurus, and some cannibals.

12. I believe in being subject to kings, presidents, rulers and magis. . . wait, no I don't.

13. I believe in being honest to a point, true to myself, chased by the police, benevolent to the deserving, virtuous on the Internet, and in doing whatever my wife says; indeed, I may say that I follow the admonition of Paul in believing, hoping and enduring—and that all of this damn well better be worth it in the end.

Robert Kirby was born into a military family. After completing high school he served a two-year mission in Uruguay for The Church of Jesus Christ of Latter-day Saints. Upon his return he pursued a career in law enforcement with the Grantsville, Utah Police Department in 1978 and then the Springville, Utah police department in 1979. While taking night classes at nearby Brigham Young University Kirby began writing columns for the local newspapers, first the *Springville Herald*, and later the *Utah County Journal* (writing under the pen name Officer "Blitz" Kreeg).

In 1989 Kirby decided to leave police work and devote himself to full-time writing. He has written a column for *The Salt Lake Tribune* since 1994. This is his 10th book.

Kirby is a popular convention speaker, and travels widely to appear at conventions and meetings. His newspaper columns have won several regional awards.

He's lived in Herriman, Utah since 2003. He and his wife have three daughters.

Made in the USA
Charleston, SC
07 November 2014